W9-ATN-439

Here's all the great literature in this grade level of *Celebrate Reading!*
Books A–D
MARTIN LUTHER KING, JR.
I HAVE A DREAM
WRITINGS AND SPEECHES THAT CHANGED THE WORLD
FOREWORD BY CORETTA SCOTT KING
Anne Frank
The Diary
Young Girl
Hatchet
GARY PAULSEN
ROOTS
The Saga of an American Family
ALEX HALEY

THE
JOY LUCK
CLUB
AMY TAN
ROOTS
The Saga of an American Family
ALEX
HALEY
MY
SWEETHEART
?
North
America
Europe
South
America
Africa
Australia

Mirror, Mirror

And Other Reflections

Triumph of the Human Spirit

Meeting Challenges

Book B Celebrate Reading!

The Outside Shot
from the novel by Walter Dean Myers
✷ Parents' Choice Award

The Treasure of Lemon Brown
from the collection by Walter Dean Myers

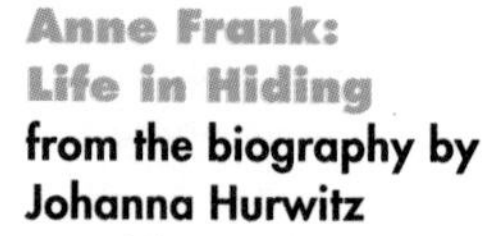

Anne Frank: Life in Hiding
from the biography by Johanna Hurwitz
✷ Notable Social Studies Trade Book

The Diary of Anne Frank
from the play by Frances Goodrich and Albert Hackett
✷ Pulitzer Prize for Drama

The Diary of a Young Girl
by Anne Frank

Dream Poems
by Langston Hughes
✷ Spingarn Medal Author

Sweetgrass
from the novel by Jan Hudson
✷ ALA Best Book for Young Adults
✷ Notable Social Studies Trade Book

Hatchet
from the novel by Gary Paulsen
✷ Newbery Honor Book
✷ Notable Social Studies Trade Book

Featured Poets
Langston Hughes
Eve Merriam
Tony Moreno

Searching for Who You Are

You Have Seen Our Faces

Stories About America

Book D Celebrate Reading!

Shades of Gray
from the novel by Carolyn Reeder
- ALA Notable Children's Book
- Young Adults' Choice

The Boys' War
from the book by Jim Murphy
- Golden Kite Award

The Incredible Journey of Lewis and Clark
from the book by Rhoda Blumberg
- ALA Notable Children's Book

Streams to the River, River to the Sea
from the novel by Scott O'Dell
- Parents' Choice

An Illustrated History of the Chinese in America
from the book by Ruthanne Lum McCunn

Tales from Gold Mountain: Stories of the Chinese in the New World
from the collection by Paul Yee
- Notable Social Studies Trade Book

Crow and Weasel
from the novel by Barry Lopez

American Women: Their Lives in Their Words
from the book by Doreen Rappaport
- Notable Social Studies Trade Book

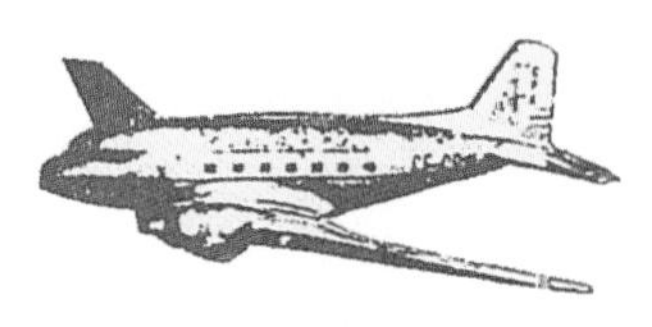

The Promised Land
from the book by Mary Antin

I Have a Dream
by Martin Luther King, Jr.

Always to Remember: The Story of the Vietnam Veterans Memorial
from the book by Brent Ashabranner
✷ ALA Notable Children's Book

Featured Poets
Walt Whitman
Emma Lazarus
Carl Sandburg

Trade Books Celebrate Reading!

More Great Books to Read!

Queen of Hearts
by Vera and Bill Cleaver

Julie of the Wolves
by Jean Craighead George

After the Dancing Days
by Margaret Rostkowski

Prairie Songs
by Pam Conrad

Jacob Have I Loved
by Katerine Paterson

The Upstairs Room
by Johanna Reiss

The Mouse Rap
by Walter Dean Myers

Shark Beneath the Reef
by Jean Craighead George

Triumph

of the Human Spirit

Meeting Challenges

Titles in This Set

The Cover Story
David Diaz illustrated the cover and title pages in his unique style by adding watercolor and dyes to silk screen prints. He remembers that art was more interesting than vowels even in first grade, when he filled in the worksheet "N__SE" with the picture of a nose and face. David has known since then how important art is to him.

ISBN: 0-673-80083-0

Acknowledgments appear on page 144.

45678910RRS99989796959493

Triumph

of the Human Spirit

Meeting Challenges

ScottForesman
A Division of HarperCollins*Publishers*

Contents

Langston Hughes's Dreams

Survival!

Student Resources

eddie

by
Walter Dean Myers

Playing basketball in Harlem playgrounds had been comfortable, sure. Lonnie had known the people, the scene, and just how good his game was. Now, at a college nearly a thousand miles from home, he just didn't seem to fit in. It was a bad feeling, a feeling that Lonnie shared with little Eddie Brignole.

They give me this little piece of job. I was supposed to work in a hospital which was about a mile away from the campus. It was called University Hospital. A lot of the kids who were studying to be doctors and whatnot, they worked in the hospital. What I was supposed to do was to work in the physical therapy department. Leeds said there wasn't much to the job, but I had to do it if I wanted to get some money for extra expenses, 'cause the scholarship only covered books and tuition and stuff and just enough money to get by on.

got the campus bus and went over to the hospital. I found the physical therapy department after asking about six people directions. They looked at me as if they had never seen a black guy before. Finally they sent me down to the end of the building that looked a little newer than the rest.

"Excuse me, I'm supposed to see Dr. Corbett."

The woman sitting behind the desk was kind of nice-looking. I thought I had seen her around the campus before but I wasn't too sure.

"You're Lonnie Jackson?" she asked. "The basketball player?"

"Yeah."

"I'm Ann Taylor." She stuck out her hand and I shook it. "It's really Annie Taylor, but I hate

Annie, okay?"

"Hey, mama, it's your name."

"I hate mama, too."

"Yes, ma'am."

"Okay. Dr. Corbett isn't here right now, he's usually here in the mornings. It's my understanding that you're only going to be here six hours a week, right?"

"Right. Two days, three hours each day."

"Okay. Eddie Brignole comes twice a week, two and a half hours each time. I think you can work with him."

"*You* think?"

"Dr. Corbett isn't too enthusiastic about the athletes working with the kids, but we're too shorthanded to complain, really."

"Yeah, right."

"Let me tell you about Eddie. He's got one real problem, as far as we know. Sometimes with a kid you really can't tell what problems they have until they're more developed. Anyway, Eddie's nine and he's so withdrawn that at first we thought he was autistic, you know what I mean?"

"What does he do, draw and stuff like that?"

"Draw?" She had pretty eyes, man, and when she said that they got kind of wide and nice.

"No, he doesn't draw. He just sits around and does nothing most of the time. He won't play with the other kids or anything. Most of the time he just goes into the gym and sits by himself. What we do is just sit with him and talk to him. The staff psychiatrist seems to think that he looks forward to coming here even if he doesn't do anything and that it might help in the long run. Once in a while the athletes do get a rise from him, but not usually. So there you are."

"You said he'll be here soon?"

"Oh, one more little problem that you'll just love," Ann said. "Can I call you Lonnie?"

"Yeah."

"Eddie comes here with his mother. She sits in the gymnasium for the whole time. Whatever you do will be wrong as far as she is concerned. If she had the money she would take him to the—how does she put it now—'the best clinics in the world.' But she doesn't, so she's stuck with us, and we're stuck with her. She's not shy about telling you either."

"Okay," I said. "I guess I can handle it."

"I hope so. She's worn out two football players already."

I just sat around for a while and read and looked at a magazine until this kid Eddie was supposed to show up. After a while a woman about medium height with dark hair pulled away from her face with a comb and bobby pins at the back of her head came in. She wore a suede jacket with fur trim that fit her kind of nice. She probably could have looked a little better if she took care of herself. Ann motioned for me to come over. Well, this chick was sitting at the side of Ann's desk drumming her fingers like she was angry already.

"Mrs. Brignole, this is Lonnie Jackson." Ann's voice carried a smile with it. "He's going to be working with Eddie for a while."

"Hello." I stuck out my hand. She looked at it, and when she looked back at Ann she didn't make a move to shake my hand.

"Does he have experience working with young children?" she asked.

"Not at all," Ann said, smiling. "But I'm sure he'll do a wonderful job, Mrs. Brignole."

"If he has no experience, I don't want him working with Eddie," Mrs. Brignole said. "I insist upon having someone with some experience at least."

"Fine," Ann said. "We might get some experienced people in when the new budget is approved next spring. If and when we do, you'll be the first person we contact."

"I think . . . I think you're being impudent," Mrs. Brignole said.

"If you want to speak to Dr. Corbett, it's fine with me," Ann said. "He'll be in sometime tomorrow morning."

Mrs. Brignole took a deep breath and put her fingertips to her brow. Ann looked at her and then looked down at the desk. I started to say something like how I would try real hard, but Ann stopped me by raising her hand. I wasn't that interested in working with a handicapped kid in the first place.

"What am I supposed to do?" Mrs. Brignole spat each word out carefully. "Give my son over to any student who seems to have nothing to do?"

"I'm sorry, Mrs. Brignole," Ann said. "The

only thing I can do is offer you what services we have. I don't want to sound uncaring, because I'm not, but you're going to have to take what we have to offer or wait until our budget is increased. Look, why don't you go and get Eddie, at least for today, and let him meet Lonnie."

Mrs. Brignole took a deep breath, stood, and walked out of the office.

"She don't seem too happy to see me," I said.

"She is not a happy woman," Ann answered.

"Look, is that it, she's just going now?"

"No, she has Eddie out in the car. She has this station wagon that looks like a World War Two tank. You know, the child has been like this for a long, long time. It's got to be hard on her, too, Lonnie. Dr. Corbett thinks it would help if she went through a little therapy herself, but she won't do it."

"She's a little wacky?" Lonnie asked.

"Probably not your out-and-out wack," Ann said. "But the home environment isn't right. A few hours here isn't going to help very much. But at least Eddie hasn't gotten worse."

"What do you do when he comes here? I mean, does he have a program?"

"No, he sits on the floor and he stays there for the whole time unless there's a chair set up—then he sits on that."

"He sits down wherever you put the chair?"

"Wherever you put it," Ann said.

"Hey, look, what am I supposed to be doing with the dude?"

"Well, let him sit down on the chair and you could talk to him and you can do jumping jacks, anything. He will just look at you. If he responds to anything, which I don't think he will, then you can try to play on that. The whole thing is to try to get some response and, you know, other than that, you're just baby-sitting."

"Yeah, okay. Look, I'm going to check on the gym."

I went into the gym. It was a little dinky gym. I saw where the chairs were stacked against the one wall and I got one. I set it up and put it at the side of the foul lane under one basket. I saw a basketball and I went and got that.

Just then a door opened and Mrs. Brignole came in with Eddie. He was a little kid. Not even five feet tall. He looked a lot like his mother, except for his hair. Her hair was dark brown and his was like a red, a deep, dark red. I stood beneath the basket, just sort of bouncing the ball off the backboard. I watched as Eddie came slowly toward the chair and sat in it. Mrs. Brignole leaned against the wall.

"Do you want to sit there or do you want to get up and play some ball?" I asked.

Nothing.

The cat's face wasn't like blank, which is what

I thought that Ann meant. Instead he just had his head down, like, you know, beaten, pushed down. I threw the basketball through the hoop and I looked at Eddie. The boy's head was still down.

"Okay," I said. "Now you sitting in that chair because somebody told you that you got to sit in that chair, right?"

Nothing.

"Now you got to look at what I'm doing for the same reason you got to sit in that chair, because if you don't look at me, then I don't know if you know what I'm doing, see. And you and me are going to get along. You can't make believe I ain't here. That's the only thing I don't like. Now you look at me, man."

Nothing.

Eddie kept his head down.

"Hey, I'm not going to keep telling you. When I tell you to look at me, I'm serious, man. I'm really serious."

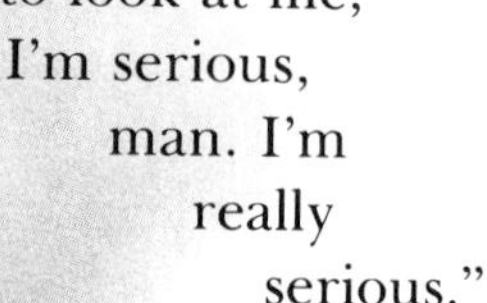

Nothing.

I put the ball under my arm and walked over to the dude and lifted his chin up. I moved my arm and he let his head fall down to his chest again. I lifted it up again, the expression was the same. Now, I mean, he looked like he was sad, so I lifted his head a little harder.

"Hey, man, stop ignoring me, man."

Out of the corner of my eye I could see his mama changing her position. I stood back and watched as my man's head dropped again and then I passed him the ball. It bounced lightly off his chest. I grabbed the ball and went up for a layup.

"Two nothing, my favor," I said. "Now it's your turn." I bounced the ball off of him again. "You missed an inbound pass, dude," I said, grabbing the ball. "I got it, I'll dribble around you, fake you out, and shoot. Yes! I got the ball in, that's four points for me and nothing for you. I'm going to wipe you up, turkey, you ain't no ballplayer."

I bounced the ball off Eddie's leg this time, grabbed it off the ground and started dribbling around him, faking left and faking right, then I leaned against Eddie's chair and turned around and put up a soft hook that touched nothing but net and fell through.

"All right. The kid is on his game," I said. "The television cameras are on me as I slaughter you, Eddieee. The score, nothing for you and six for meee."

I saw his mother take a step forward and stop. I see she is one of those protective mamas. I didn't care. I backed off a little bit and threw the ball to him, lightly.

"Here comes a pass to you." Bang. He didn't move and the ball rolled over to the side. I grabbed it.

"I got the rebound, now I'm going to dribble around you again and I'm going to fake you out. Here I come." I dribbled past him and laid the ball up again. "There, man. That's *ten* for me and nothing for you."

"Eight," came the voice from Eddie Brignole. "You only have eight."

"Okay, turkey," I said. "Eight. I thought I could beat you a little easier than that. I see you watching everything I do, huh. Okay, this time I'm not going to announce the game, man. I'm just going to go on and shoot the ball, man. 'Cause you got your head down and you won't be seeing what I be doing, man. Okay, here comes the ball to you." I threw him the ball. It bounced off of him again. I grabbed it and moved toward the basket, but this time I was watching him and he turned just as I threw the ball against the backboard. It fell through.

"Now I got ten, now I got ten!" Then I came back, threw him the ball again. I saw his hand move, he wanted to grab it. I just knew he wanted to grab that ball.

I said, "Okay, okay, Eddie, now the game is twenty. I got ten in the first half. But right now I'm going to show you a few shots, right? I'm going to amaze you. Watch this."

I moved back to the top of the key. I looked at him to see if he was looking at me. He wasn't looking right at me but he had lifted his head and I knew he could see me out of the corner of his eye. I put the ball on the floor one time and I threw up a soft jump shot. It arched easily through the air and bounced off the back rim. I looked over at Eddie and he smiled.

"Hey, man, don't be smiling at me. I mean, I could still beat you, even if I did miss that one shot."

It went on like that for about a half hour more. The dude was actually glad to see me miss and I didn't care. It was like a little game we were playing. He was sitting there watching me, hoping I would miss and I was watching him, seeing how he would react. Then I told him we would have a rest period and we would start the second half of our game, but this time I told him I wanted him to get up off that chair and try a shot. All you got to do is try one shot, just one shot and that's all, okay, one shot?

"Can you make one shot? Oh, I see you can't even make one shot, that's your problem, man."

He didn't say anything. I sort of picked him up in one arm, half lifted him, and walked him over to the basket. I knew he could walk okay. I put the basketball in his hands and lifted it, and I told him very softly in his ear, "Don't drop this ball when I give it to you, man. Don't drop this ball, 'cause I ain't like those other people, man, you know. I'm black and mean, jim. So don't drop this basketball."

I put it in his hand and he held it for a long moment.

"Go on shoot it, go on shoot it."

e threw the ball up, it hit the bottom of the rim and fell down. I grabbed it and I kept on playing like I had before when he was sitting down. I would grab it and dribble around him. He just stood there. I kept throwing him the ball but he would just let it bounce off his body.

I said, "Okay, man."

I figured I would see what this dude was really made of. I had an idea what he was made of when I saw the smile when I missed the shot and when he corrected me on the score. The dude didn't like losing. He didn't like losing, I knew.

I said, "Okay, Eddie, tell you what I'm going

to do, man. Since I'm on the basketball team and you're not even on a basketball team, I guess you need a little break, so I'm going to give you a break. Here, I'm going to give you the basketball and walk all the way across the gym now. If you make a basket before I get back over to you, I'm going to give you ten points. Now hold this basketball, Eddie, HOLD THE BASKETBALL. I told you I'm black and mean, jim."

He took the basketball. I didn't have to lift his arms. I walked all the way across the floor, turned, and said, "Okay, Eddie, here I come now." I began walking slowly toward him. He didn't move. I kept on coming, very slowly. "Here I come, Eddie, here I come. You better get it up now. You better get it up. If you want them ten points you better get it up, here I come."

"Don't intimidate him."

This is from his mother. She started from the other direction.

"She must be on your side, Eddie. Here she comes to help you."

She moved faster and I moved faster. Eddie shifted his feet. "Don't intimidate him, don't intimidate my son. You don't know a thing about . . ."

I jumped in front of her as she neared her son. She tried to get around me, but I kept blocking her out, blocking her out.

"She must be on your side."

"What are you doing? Are you crazy . . . are you cra— What are you doing?"

"I know you want to pass the ball to her, Eddie, but I won't let you do it, man. I'm not going to let you do it, man."

"You get out of my way."

Eddie turned and threw the ball up against the backboard. The ball rolled around the rim and I said a quick, quick prayer. "Lord, PLEASE, let it roll in."

The Lord did a cool thing, as the ball fell through the hoop.

Eddie looked up at the basket and then he glanced over at me.

"Good shot," I said. "You got a nice touch."

I went and got the ball. Eddie's mother stood still for a long moment in the middle of the floor, and then she went back to where she had been standing near the wall. I didn't try to force Eddie to shoot anymore, and he didn't. Once, when the ball landed near him, he picked it up, held it for a second or two, and then threw it to me.

I felt relaxed with Eddie. I felt like just hanging around the gym with him and shooting baskets. I didn't know exactly how Eddie felt, but I knew that at that moment, standing in a gym in Indiana, he wasn't feeling great about himself. I knew the feeling.

1 If you were in charge, what would you do to help Eddie?

2 Why is Eddie so quiet? Find clues to help you explain.

3 Both Eddie and Eddie's mother are asked at the end of the day to evaluate Lonnie's handling of Eddie. How does Eddie rank him? How about Eddie's mother? Explain.

The Treasure of Lemon Brown

by
Walter Dean
Myers

The dark sky, filled with angry, swirling clouds, reflected Greg Ridley's mood as he sat on the stoop of his building. His father's voice came to him again, first reading the letter the principal had sent to the house, then lecturing endlessly about his poor efforts in math.

"I had to leave school when I was thirteen," his father had said, "that's a year younger than you are now. If I'd had half the chances that you have, I'd . . ."

Greg had sat in the small, pale green kitchen listening, knowing the lecture would end with his father saying he couldn't play ball with the Scorpions. He had asked his father the week before, and his father had said it depended on his next report card. It wasn't often the Scorpions took on new players, especially fourteen-year-olds, and this was a chance of a lifetime for Greg. He hadn't been allowed to play high school ball, which he had really wanted to do, but playing for the Community Center team was the next best thing. Report cards were due in a week, and Greg had been hoping for the best. But the principal had ended the suspense early when she sent that letter saying Greg would probably fail math if he didn't spend more time studying.

"And you want to play *basketball?*" His father's brows knitted over deep brown eyes. "That must be some kind of a joke. Now you just get into your room and hit those books."

That had been two nights before. His father's words, like the distant thunder that now echoed through the streets of Harlem, still rumbled softly in his ears.

It was beginning to cool. Gusts of wind made bits of paper dance between the parked cars. There was a flash of nearby lightning, and soon large drops of rain splashed onto his jeans. He stood to go upstairs, thought of the lecture that probably awaited him if he did anything except shut himself in his room with his math book, and started walking down the street instead. Down the block there was an old tenement that had been abandoned for some months. Some of the guys had held an impromptu checker tournament there the week before, and Greg had noticed that the door, once boarded over, had been slightly ajar.

Pulling his collar up as high as he could, he checked for traffic and made a dash across the street. He reached the house just as another flash of lightning changed the night to day for an instant, then returned the graffiti-scarred building to the grim shadows. He vaulted over the outer stairs and pushed tentatively on the door. It was open, and he let himself in.

The inside of the building was dark except for the dim light that filtered through the dirty windows from the streetlamps. There was a room a few feet from the door, and from where he stood at the entrance, Greg could see a squarish patch of light on the floor. He entered the room, frowning at the musty smell. It was a large room that might have been someone's parlor at one time. Squinting, Greg could see an old table on its side against one wall, what looked like a pile of rags or a torn mattress in the corner, and a couch, with one side broken, in front of the window.

He went to the couch. The side that wasn't broken was comfortable enough, though a little creaky. From this spot he could see the blinking neon sign over the bodega on the corner. He sat awhile, watching the sign blink first green then red, allowing his mind to drift to the Scorpions, then to his father. His father had been a postal worker for all Greg's life, and was proud of it, often telling Greg how hard he had worked to pass the test. Greg had heard the story too many times to be interested now.

For a moment Greg thought he heard something that sounded like a scraping against the wall. He listened carefully, but it was gone.

Outside the wind had picked up, sending the rain against the window with a force that shook the glass in its frame. A car passed, its tires hissing over the wet street and its red taillights glowing in the darkness.

Greg thought he heard the noise again. His stomach tightened as he held himself still and listened intently. There weren't any more scraping noises, but he was sure he had heard something in the darkness—something breathing!

e tried to figure out just where the breathing was coming from; he knew it was in the room with him. Slowly he stood, tensing. As he turned, a flash of lightning lit up the room, frightening him with its sudden brilliance. He saw nothing, just the overturned table, the pile of rags and an old newspaper on the floor. Could he have been imagining the sounds? He continued listening, but heard nothing and thought that it might have just been rats. Still, he thought, as soon as the rain let up he would leave. He went to the window and was about to look out when he heard a voice behind him.

"Don't try nothin' 'cause I got a razor here sharp enough to cut a week into nine days!"

Greg, except for an involuntary tremor in his knees, stood stock still. The voice was high and brittle, like dry twigs being broken, surely not one he had ever heard before. There was a shuffling sound as the person who had been speaking moved a step closer. Greg turned, holding his breath, his eyes straining to see in the dark room.

The upper part of the figure before him was still in darkness. The lower half was in the dim rectangle of light that fell unevenly from the window. There were two feet, in cracked, dirty shoes from which rose legs that were wrapped in rags.

"Who are you?" Greg hardly recognized his own voice.

"I'm Lemon Brown," came the answer. "Who're you?"

"Greg Ridley."

"What you doing here?" The figure shuffled forward again, and Greg took a small step backward.

"It's raining," Greg said.

"I can see that," the figure said.

The person who called himself Lemon Brown peered forward, and Greg could see him clearly. He was an old man. His black, heavily wrinkled face was surrounded by a halo of crinkly white hair and whiskers that seemed to separate his head from the layers of dirty coats piled on his smallish frame. His pants were bagged to the knee, where they were met with rags that went down to the old shoes. The rags were held on with strings, and there was a rope around his middle. Greg relaxed. He had seen the man before, picking through the trash on the corner and pulling clothes out of a Salvation Army box. There was no sign of the razor that could "cut a week into nine days."

"What are you doing here?" Greg asked.

"This is where I'm staying," Lemon Brown said. "What you here for?"

"Told you it was raining out," Greg said, leaning against the back of the couch until he felt it give slightly.

"Ain't you got no home?"

"I got a home," Greg answered.

"You ain't one of them bad boys looking for my treasure, is you?" Lemon Brown cocked his head to one side and squinted one eye. "Because I told you I got me a razor."

"I'm not looking for your treasure," Greg answered, smiling. "*If* you have one."

"What you mean, *if* I have one," Lemon Brown said. "Every man got a treasure. You don't know that, you must be a fool!"

"Sure," Greg said as he sat on the sofa and put one leg over the back. "What do you have, gold coins?"

"Don't worry none about what I got," Lemon Brown said. "You know who I am?"

"You told me your name was orange or lemon or something like that."

"Lemon Brown," the old man said, pulling back his shoulders as he did so, "they used to call me Sweet Lemon Brown."

"Sweet Lemon?" Greg asked.

"Yessir. Sweet Lemon Brown. They used to say I sung the blues so sweet that if I sang at a funeral, the dead would commence to rocking with the beat. Used to travel all over Mississippi and as far as Monroe, Louisiana, and east on over to Macon, Georgia. You mean you ain't never heard of Sweet Lemon Brown?"

"Afraid not," Greg said. "What . . . what happened to you?"

"Hard times, boy. Hard times always after a poor man. One day I got tired, sat down to rest a spell and felt a tap on my shoulder. Hard times caught up with me."

"Sorry about that."

"What you doing here? How come you didn't go on home when the rain come? Rain don't bother you young folks none."

"Just didn't." Greg looked away.

"I used to have a knotty-headed boy just like you." Lemon Brown had half walked, half shuffled back to the corner and sat down against the wall. "Had them big eyes like you got. I used to call them moon eyes. Look into them moon eyes and see anything you want."

"How come you gave up singing the blues?" Greg asked.

"Didn't give it up," Lemon Brown said. "You don't give up the blues; they give you up. After a while you do good for yourself, and it ain't nothing but foolishness singing about how hard you got it. Ain't that right?"

"I guess so."

"What's that noise?" Lemon Brown asked, suddenly sitting upright.

Greg listened, and he heard a noise outside. He looked at Lemon Brown and saw the old man was pointing toward the window.

Greg went to the window and saw three men, neighborhood thugs, on the stoop. One was carrying a length of pipe. Greg looked back toward Lemon Brown, who moved quietly across the room to the window. The old man looked out, then beckoned frantically for Greg to follow him. For a moment Greg couldn't move. Then he found himself following Lemon Brown into the hallway and up darkened stairs. Greg followed as closely as he could. They reached the top of the stairs, and Greg felt Lemon Brown's hand first lying on his shoulder, then probing down his arm until he finally took Greg's hand into his own as they crouched in the darkness.

"They's bad men," Lemon Brown whispered. His breath was warm against Greg's skin.

"Hey! Rag man!" A voice called. "We know you in here. What you got up under them rags? You got any money?"

Silence.

"We don't want to have to come in and hurt you, old man, but we don't mind if we have to."

Lemon Brown squeezed Greg's hand in his own hard, gnarled fist.

There was a banging downstairs and a light as the men entered. They banged around noisily, calling for the rag man.

"We heard you talking about your treasure." The voice was slurred. "We just want to see it, that's all."

"You sure he's here?" One voice seemed to come from the room with the sofa.

"Yeah, he stays here every night."

"There's another room over there; I'm going to take a look. You got that flashlight?"

"Yeah, here, take the pipe too."

Greg opened his mouth to quiet the sound of his breath as he sucked it in uneasily. A beam of light hit the wall a few feet opposite him, then went out.

"Ain't nobody in that room," a voice said. "You think he gone or something?"

"I don't know," came the answer. "All I know is that I heard him talking about some kind of treasure. You know they found that shopping bag lady with that money in her bags."

"Yeah. You think he's upstairs?"

"HEY, OLD MAN, ARE YOU UP THERE?"

Silence.

"Watch my back, I'm going up."

There was a footstep on the stairs, and the beam from the flashlight danced crazily along the peeling wallpaper. Greg held his breath. There was another step and a loud crashing noise as the man banged the pipe against the wooden banister. Greg could feel his temples throb as the man slowly neared them. Greg thought about the pipe, wondering what he would do when the man reached them—what he *could* do.

Then Lemon Brown released his hand and moved toward the top of the stairs. Greg looked around and saw stairs going up to the next floor. He tried waving to Lemon Brown, hoping the old man would see him in the dim light and follow him to the next floor. Maybe, Greg thought, the man wouldn't follow them up there. Suddenly, though, Lemon Brown stood at the top of the stairs, both arms raised high above his head.

"There he is!" A voice cried from below.

"Throw down your money, old man, so I won't have to bash your head in!"

Lemon Brown didn't move. Greg felt himself near panic. The steps came closer, and still Lemon Brown didn't move. He was an eerie sight, a bundle of rags standing at the top of the stairs, his shadow on the wall looming over him. Maybe, the thought came to Greg, the scene could be even eerier.

Greg wet his lips, put his hands to his mouth and tried to make a sound. Nothing came out. He swallowed hard, wet his lips once more and howled as evenly as he could.

"What's that?"

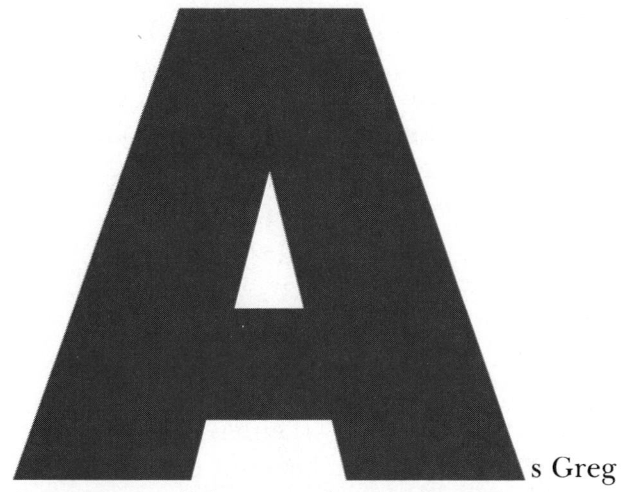

s Greg howled, the light moved away from Lemon Brown, but not before Greg saw him hurl his body down the stairs at the men who had come to take his treasure. There was a crashing noise, and then footsteps. A rush of warm air came in as the downstairs door opened, then there was only an ominous silence.

Greg stood on the landing. He listened, and after a while there was another sound on the staircase.

"Mr. Brown?" he called.

"Yeah, it's me," came the answer. "I got their flashlight."

Greg exhaled in relief as Lemon Brown made his way slowly back up the stairs.

"You OK?"

"Few bumps and bruises," Lemon Brown said.

"I think I'd better be going," Greg said, his breath returning to normal. "You'd better leave, too, before they come back."

"They may hang around outside for a while," Lemon Brown said, "but they ain't getting their nerve up to come in here again. Not with crazy old rag men and howling spooks. Best you stay a while till the coast is clear. I'm heading out west tomorrow, out to east St. Louis."

"They were talking about treasures," Greg said. "You *really* have a treasure?"

"What I tell you? Didn't I tell you every man got a treasure?" Lemon Brown said. "You want to see mine?"

"If you want to show it to me," Greg shrugged.

"Let's look out the window first, see what them scoundrels be doing," Lemon Brown said.

They followed the oval beam of the flashlight into one of the rooms and looked out the window. They saw the men who had tried to take the treasure sitting on the curb near the corner. One of them had his pants leg up, looking at his knee.

"You sure you're not hurt?" Greg asked Lemon Brown.

"Nothing that ain't been hurt before," Lemon Brown said. "When you get as old as me all you say when something hurts is, 'Howdy, Mr. Pain, sees you back again.' Then when Mr. Pain see he can't worry you none, he go on mess with somebody else."

Greg smiled.

"Here, you hold this." Lemon Brown gave Greg the flashlight.

He sat on the floor near Greg and carefully untied the strings that held the rags on his right leg. When he took the rags away, Greg saw a piece of plastic. The old man carefully took off the plastic and unfolded it. He revealed some yellowed newspaper clippings and a battered harmonica.

"There it be," he said, nodding his head.

"There it be."

Greg looked at the old man, saw the distant look in his eye, then turned to the clippings. They told of Sweet Lemon Brown, a blues singer and harmonica player who was appearing at different theaters in the South. One of the clippings said he had been the hit of the show, although not the headliner. All of the clippings were reviews of shows Lemon Brown had been in more than 50 years ago. Greg looked at the harmonica. It was dented badly on one side, with the reed holes on one end nearly closed.

"I used to travel around and make money for to feed my wife and Jesse—that's my boy's name. Used to feed them good, too. Then his mama died, and he stayed with his mama's sister. He growed up to be a man, and when the war come he saw fit to go off and fight in it. I didn't have nothing to give him except these things that told him who I was, and what he come from. If you know your pappy did something, you know you can do something too.

"Anyway, he went off to war, and I went off still playing and singing. 'Course by then I wasn't as much as I used to be, not without somebody to make it worth the while. You know what I mean?"

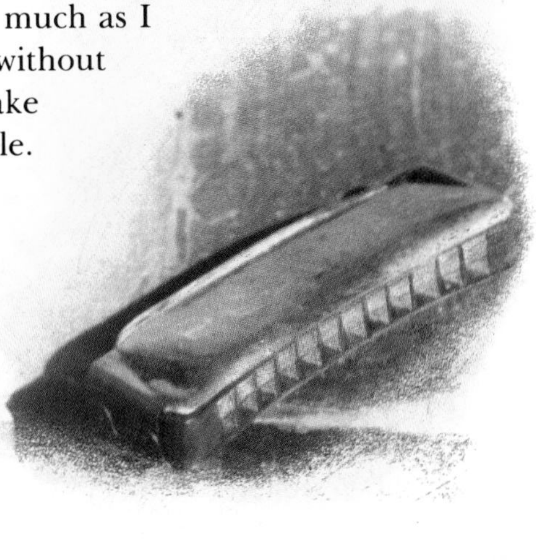

"Yeah," Greg nodded, not quite really knowing.

"I traveled around, and one time I come home, and there was this letter saying Jesse got killed in the war. Broke my heart, it truly did.

"They sent back what he had with him over there, and what it was is this old mouth fiddle and these clippings. Him carrying it around with him like that told me it meant something to him. That was my treasure, and when I give it to him he treated it just like that, a treasure. Ain't that something?"

"Yeah, I guess so," Greg said.

"You *guess* so?" Lemon Brown's voice rose an octave as he started to put his treasure back into the plastic. "Well, you got to guess 'cause you sure don't know nothing. Don't know enough to get home when it's raining."

"I guess . . . I mean, you're right."

"You OK for a youngster," the old man said as he tied the strings around his leg, "better than those scalawags what come here looking for my treasure. That's for sure."

"You really think that treasure of yours was worth fighting for?" Greg asked. "Against a pipe?"

"What else a man got 'cepting what he can pass on to his son, or his daughter, if she be his oldest?" Lemon Brown said. "For a big-headed boy you sure do ask the foolishest questions."

Lemon Brown got up after patting his rags in place and looked out the window again.

"Looks like they're gone. You get on out of here and get yourself home. I'll be watching from the window so you'll be all right."

Lemon Brown went down the stairs behind Greg. When they reached the front door the old man looked out first, saw the street was clear and told Greg to scoot on home.

"You sure you'll be OK?" Greg asked.

"Now didn't I tell you I was going to east St. Louis in the morning?" Lemon Brown asked. "Don't that sound OK to you?"

"Sure it does," Greg said. "Sure it does. And you take care of that treasure of yours."

"That I'll do," Lemon said, the wrinkles about his eyes suggesting a smile. "That I'll do."

The night had warmed and the rain had stopped, leaving puddles at the curbs. Greg didn't even want to think how late it was. He thought ahead of what his father would say and wondered if he should tell him about Lemon Brown. He thought about it until he reached his stoop, and decided against it. Lemon Brown would be OK, Greg thought, with his memories and his treasure.

Greg pushed the button over the bell marked Ridley, thought of the lecture he knew his father would give him, and smiled.

A WORD FROM THE AUTHOR

writing and revising

"the treasure of lemon brown"

Myers as a teenager

by Walter Dean Myers

Walter Dean Myers

Stories in old newspapers fascinate me, especially when they are accompanied by pictures. There is a picture of a great man delivering a speech and on the edge of the crowd before him there is a child who clings to the skirt of its mother. I wonder about the child. Did she remember the speech? Did she know what happened that day? What was she thinking about?

It was this kind of feeling, this kind of wondering about people that led to "The Treasure of Lemon Brown." I had seen, in an old newspaper, an advertisement for a blues singer. The singer was a handsome young black man, smiling and neatly dressed. For a while I forgot the picture, and then it came back to me. I imagined him on stage singing before a large audience. Then I moved him, still in my imagination, to a theater in a small southern city. Now I saw him arriving in the city by bus. He carried a small suitcase which contained two shirts, underwear, and his other suit. In one corner of the suitcase, wrapped in his socks, was his harmonica.

Now I imagined him thinking about his wife and a child. What happened to his wife? What happened to his child? As the images came to me, as they were fleshed out with detail, they became the basis for "The Treasure of Lemon Brown."

To write the story, I wanted someone to discover what I had discovered, the past life of a human being. No, what I wanted was for someone to discover a human being, to see an old man, poorly dressed and homeless, and to find in him those cares and feelings that define us all as human.

"I dropped out of school when I was thirteen," the elder Ridley had said, "that's a year younger than you are now. If

I had half the chances that you have, I'd . . ."

How many times had I heard that from my father? Did he really think that I *wanted* to do badly in school? It didn't have anything to do with the fact that I wanted to play basketball with the Comanches, the neighborhood team. What my father didn't seem to realize was that I was 6′1″ and playing ball was one of the things I did best. He also didn't realize just how cool it was to play for the Comanches.

I dropped out of school became *I had to leave school. Dropping out* needed more explaining than *had to leave. The elder Ridley* became *his father*—a change in point of view and less stiff. I decided to change the name of the team from the Comanches (the smoothest basketball team in Harlem!) to the Scorpions so my friends wouldn't think the story was too personal.

I got Greg into the abandoned house and wanted to establish the odd nature of Lemon Brown. I tried to do this by describing Greg's first encounter with Lemon:

"Don't you try nothing, I got a razor here sharp enough to cut a week into nine days!"

Greg, except for an involuntary trembling in his knees, stood stock still. The voice was high and brittle, like dry twigs being broken . . .

I don't know why I changed *trembling* to *tremor. Trembling* seems better now.

Greg quickly relaxed when he saw the man was not dangerous. To convey this message, I said that Greg had seen the man before, *pulling clothes out of a Salvation Army box.* At the time I was writing the story, my son was in the Salvation Army after-school program, and I had seen people bringing clothing to put into the box. I don't think people were allowed to take clothing from the box, but I used that idea anyway.

When the bad guys showed up, they frightened Greg but Lemon stood up to them. Greg and the old man were on the same side, and while this was a sudden event, it had been foreshadowed by Greg's having seen the old man before and Lemon's comparing Greg with his own son.

After the encounter with the bad guys, Lemon showed Greg his treasure:

He sat on the floor near Greg and carefully undid the strings which held the rags around his right leg. When he had done this and taken the rags away, Greg saw that there was plastic under the rags. The old man took the plastic off and laid it carefully on the ground. He took the top layer of plastic off. There was a neat pile of yellowed newspaper clippings. Then he fished in his pocket and pulled out a battered harmonica. Lemon Brown tapped them gently with a crooked black finger.

"There it be," he said. "There it be."

Okay, so here's the beginning of my big scene, the one in which I reveal that Lemon Brown's treasure is his rich memory of his son and of the love they shared. I saw I was using the word *carefully* too much, but more importantly, I needed to get to the treasure faster. I made one sentence simpler—*When he took the rags away, Greg saw a piece of plastic.* Then, instead of having the harmonica in his pocket (which suggests he might still play it and might even play it for Greg), I moved it into the package.

Greg had seen the treasure, had understood the love between Lemon and

Lemon's son, and now had to return home. He asked Lemon if he was going to be OK, and Lemon answered that he was going to East St. Louis in the morning, and didn't that seem OK? I noticed that one of the copy editors changed *East St. Louis,* which is in Illinois, to *east St. Louis,* which is in Missouri. Oh, well.

The original continued:

"Yeah," Greg said. "Sure it does. And you take care of that treasure of yours."

The night was cool, cooler than it had been. He didn't even want to think about how late it was. He thought ahead of what his father would say, and wondered if he should tell him about Lemon Brown.

No, I wanted the story to have a more upbeat ending than this. I've left Lemon with a smile in the final version:

"That I'll do," Lemon said, the wrinkles about his eyes suggesting a smile. "That I'll do."

Good. And for some reason, it's warm instead of cold:

The night had warmed and the rain had stopped, leaving puddles at the curbs. Greg didn't even want to think how late it was . . .

I think I'm happy with these revisions.

thinking

about it

1 Lemon Brown's treasure was important because it helped explain who he was to his son. What item or items would you call your treasure? Why are they your treasure?

2 Suppose that Walter Dean Myers visits your school. During lunch, he walks over to your table with his tray. He says, "I want to write a story about your school. What should I write about?" What would be your reply, and why?

3 Years later, Greg talks about Lemon Brown: "the effect Lemon Brown has had upon my life." What is that effect? What, who has Greg become?

Another Book by Walter Dean Myers

Me, Mop, and the Moondance Kid—what a trio of characters! As the orphanage they're living in starts to close, T. J. and Moondance get adopted, but Mop becomes a "leftover." Mop needs a family—quick! Baseball seems the only answer!

Wealth

You asked me
if i knew of
a way for you
to become rich

with something
that has never
been done
before.

Well,

if you could
teach a bullfrog
how to dance
un merengue

or compose
an orchestra
from crickets
with a
butterfly
conducting

or teach
a hawk
to sing
un guaguanco.

If you could
teach a broken
man
to smile

or if you
bottled rainbows
and gave them to
the somber
for a smile

If you could
teach
a leader
how to say
peace!
and mean it,

then i think
you would be
rich.

It's hard to do
something
that no one
has done
before . . .

by Tony Moreno

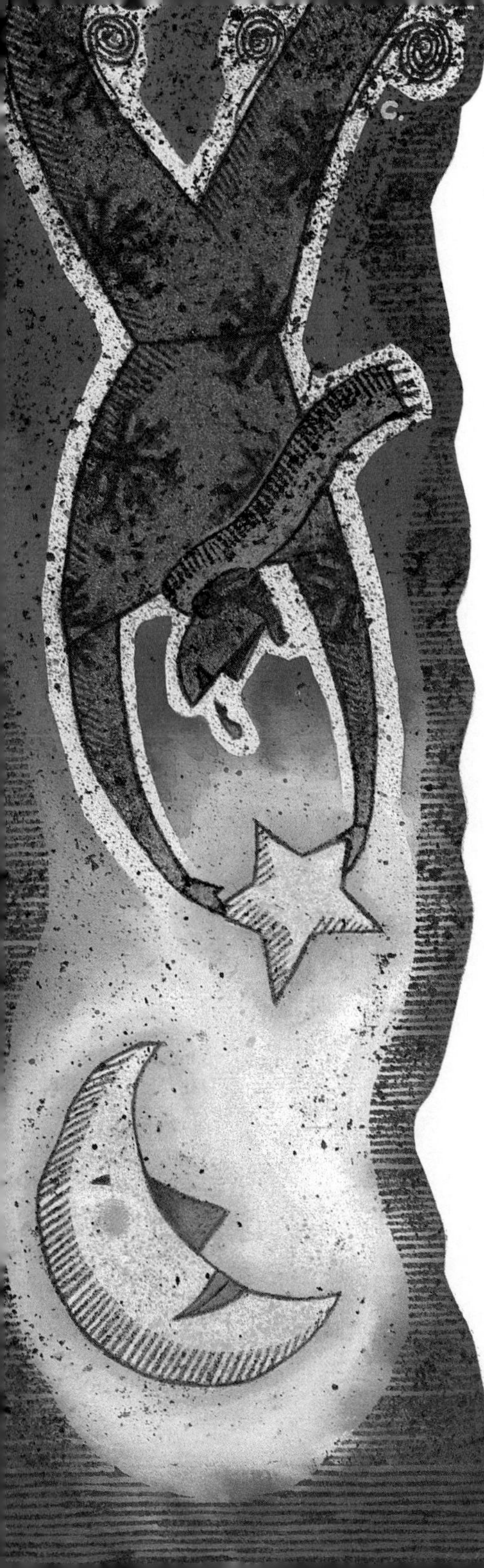

First Star

Coming home
    after school
on this late
    winter afternoon
my fingers are tingling
    inside my woolen gloves
I have to keep wriggling
    my toes
    inside my heavy boots
my breath is visible
    in the air
    like tiny jet plane trails
and I'm hugging my
    books to keep warm

the sky is already dark
I can see the first star
I'm making a wish
that on Saturday night
when I get up to dance
no one will clap
and no one will groan
they'll all just take me
    for granted
as though I've
    always been
part of the crowd

by Eve Merriam

HAPPY BIRTHDAY, ANNE

by Johanna Hurwitz

[*Anne Frank with her family and friends*]

JUNE 12, 1942, WAS THE THIRTEENTH birthday of Anne Frank. Her home, at 37 Merwede Square in Amsterdam, was filled with flowers as Anne sat down to open her presents. She received books, jewelry, a game, and a puzzle. There were chocolates and other candies. Anne also received some money that she could spend as she wished. Right away, Anne made up her mind. She would buy herself still another book, one about Greek and Roman mythology. Anne was a lively girl with loads of friends. She loved to go skating and to play with her classmates, but she loved reading, too. Among the gifts, there was a book with a red-and-white-checked cover. Inside, the pages were blank. It was a diary in which Anne could record her own story.

Probably, Anne also received a poem that her father had written in honor of the event. It was a family tradition, and Anne and her older sister Margot looked forward to those verses that he wrote for them on special occasions. He wrote his verses in German.

The Frank family lived in Holland, but it was only natural for Otto Frank to write his poems in German. He had been born and educated in Germany. In fact, the whole family—both parents and Anne and Margot—had been born in Germany. During the First World War, Otto Frank had served in the German army and had become a lieutenant. When Otto married Edith Hollander in 1925, they settled in Frankfurt, Germany. He assumed they would live there for the rest of their lives. After all, Otto's ancestors had lived in that city as far back as the seventeenth century. In 1926, the Franks' first daughter Margot was born. Three years later, on June 12, 1929, their second daughter was born. She was named Annelies Marie. It was a long name for a baby, and before long she was just called Anne.

Although the Frank family was German, it was also Jewish. In 1929, Frankfurt was the home of about 30,000 Jews among a total population of 540,000 people. After Berlin, it was the second largest Jewish community in all of Germany. At one time, there had been rules singling out the Jewish people and forcing them to live in a separate area called the ghetto. But since the beginning of the nineteenth century, new laws said that the Jews were equal to all other people in Germany; they could live and work as they pleased. With such a long history of acceptance and opportunity behind them, it was no wonder that the Franks looked forward to a long and happy life in Frankfurt.

But even though 1929, when Anne was born, was a time of celebrating for Otto and Edith Frank, it was not a good year for Germany. Many businesses closed, and, as a result, thousands of people were out of work. One-quarter of Frankfurt's population was unemployed.

A new political party called the National Socialist German Workers party—the Nazis—had been formed after the First World War. As times grew worse, more and more people supported this party. These supporters blamed the bad times in Germany on a weak government and on the Jews.

It was not the first time in history that the Jews were blamed for something they had not done. Anti-Semitism had come and gone before. Edith and Otto Frank and the other Jews around them hoped that, with time, this ill feeling toward them would be forgotten.

But as the economic situation got worse, the Nazis became stronger. In an election in 1933, Adolf Hitler, the party's leader, was elected as head of a government made up of several political parties. Two months later, he seized total power. All the other political parties in the country were outlawed, and those people who opposed the Nazi party were sent to prison camps.

With Hitler firmly in power, anti-Semitism became official government policy. Laws were passed that did not allow the Germans to shop in stores owned by Jews. It was forbidden for people who were not Jewish to consult a Jewish doctor or a

Jewish lawyer. Furthermore, physical attacks against Jews in the streets were common.

By mid-April, 1933, a law was passed stating that all public employees who had even one Jewish grandparent were to be fired from their jobs. Jewish teachers were not permitted to teach in the schools. As Jews lost their jobs, there was more work for pure Christian Germans. The Nazis called these Germans "Aryans."

Suddenly the Franks found that they were not Germans after all—they were Jews, and, because of that, they were hated. Most of the Jews living in Germany tried to convince themselves that these new laws would not last. How could more than a hundred years of acceptance be undone in just a few weeks? It was difficult for men who had served in their country's army and had fought for Germany in the last war to believe that they were not true citizens. Surely the madness of the Nazis was just a passing phase in German history.

Some Jews, however, realized that Germany was no longer a safe place in which to live and to raise their families. And Otto Frank was one of them. In 1933, when the Nazis seized power, he left Frankfurt and went to Amsterdam, Holland. He had often gone there on business trips. There, he set up a branch of a German company. His wife and daughters joined him months later, and a new life in a new country began for Anne and her family.

Holland is famous for its great religious tolerance and acceptance of all people. In the seventeenth century, the Pilgrims, who were to become the first American settlers, traveled first to Holland before they boarded the *Mayflower* and came to the New World. And still earlier, in 1492,

Jews fleeing from the Spanish Inquisition had also found a friendly home in Holland. By 1933, when the Frank family arrived in Amsterdam, there were more than 100,000 Jews living in Holland. Since half of that number made their home in Amsterdam, it was no wonder that some people called the city the "Jerusalem of Europe." And it was no wonder that Otto Frank was confident that he had made a wise choice in moving his family to Holland, away from the Nazis and the anti-Semitism of Germany.

To move to a new country and to learn a new language and customs are not easy. But Otto Frank's business thrived, and he made good friends among his Dutch colleagues. And Margot and Anne were so young that they adapted to their new home without problems. They learned to speak Dutch.

[*Otto Frank*]

The girls were enrolled at the Montessori School, which was just a few blocks from their home. They quickly made friends. In Anne's class, there were thirteen other Jewish children. Some were refugees from Germany, just like Anne.

Although it rains 175 days a year in Amsterdam, life was sunny and happy for Anne and her family. The good times, however, did not last. The influence of Hitler and the Nazis began to be felt outside of Germany. It was the Nazi plan to conquer all of Europe. First, Austria was taken over by Germany. Next, Czechoslovakia was conquered by the Germans and was no longer an independent country.

Then, on September 1, 1939, Germany invaded Poland. Two days later, France and Great Britain declared war on Germany.

Holland had been a neutral country during the First World War, and many Dutch people expected that during this new war Holland would again remain neutral. But the war was coming closer all the time. Within six months, Germany invaded Denmark and Norway. Then, on May 10, 1940, Germany invaded Belgium, Luxembourg, France, and Holland.

The invasion of Holland came as a complete surprise. The Dutch were unprepared to defend themselves against a country so much larger than they were. Within days, the country was forced to surrender. Holland was occupied by the Germans. Dutch government officials and the Dutch royal family fled to England.

For the rest of the Dutch people, there was no possibility of fleeing. Many Dutchmen were forced to go to Germany and work in the factories. Those who remained in Holland found themselves governed by new German laws. Just like in Germany, strict regulations that dealt with Jewish citizens were enforced. All Jews had to sew a yellow six-pointed star on their clothing.

Anne was forbidden to run errands for her mother, except between the hours of three and five o'clock in the afternoon. She could only go into stores that had the sign "Jewish shop." She could not be outside after eight o'clock at night, not even in her own garden. Anne and Margot could not go to the movies or play tennis or go swimming. They could not ride on a train, eat in a restaurant, or visit openly with their Christian friends. Wooden signs announcing "Voor Joden

Verboden" ("Forbidden for Jews") were posted almost everywhere.

Perhaps saddest of all, twelve-year-old Anne was forced to leave the Montessori School. She wept when she said good-by to her teacher. Anne and Margot enrolled in the Jewish Secondary School. Although they were joined by their Jewish classmates, they left behind many good friends. And they were well aware that this change in their education was still another of the dreadful events that were going on throughout the country, events that affected them and the other Jews in Holland. And it was all caused by the insane hatred that the German Nazis felt toward Jews.

Still, Anne's father tried hard to protect his daughters from fully realizing just how desperate the situation was for Jews. And that's why Anne's thirteenth birthday was celebrated with all the festivities that she had come to anticipate.

Anne was a good student and got along well with most of the teachers at her new school. But she often talked in class to her friends. One day, the math teacher became so irritated by Anne's constant talking that he gave her a special punishment. She had to write a composition about "a chatterbox."

Undaunted, Anne proved to her teacher that her words could flow as fluently on the page as they did when she spoke. She wrote that talking is a feminine characteristic, and although she might work to keep it under control, she did not think she could be cured. Furthermore, she wrote that her mother talked just as much as she did, and so being a chatterbox was undoubtedly an inherited characteristic.

The math teacher laughed at Anne's composition, and all was well until the next time Anne began to chatter in class. A second report was assigned, now entitled "Incurable Chatterbox." Again, Anne succeeded in filling the composition pages for her teacher. But when she still continued talking a few days later, he scolded her with disgust. "Anne, as punishment for talking, will do a composition entitled 'Quack, quack, quack, says Mrs. Natterbeak,'" he announced to the students. Everyone in Anne's math class roared with laughter, and Anne had to laugh, too. She was rescued from this ridiculous assignment by her friend Sanne, who offered to write a poem for Anne. The poem was about three baby ducklings who were bitten to death by their swan father because they chattered too much.

[*Anne Frank, age 13*]

The math teacher read the poem aloud to the class and shared it with his other classes, too. After that, he ignored Anne's chattering in class. He knew he couldn't change her.

For a girl as bright and as imaginative as Anne was and who could express herself so readily on paper, a diary was a wonderful birthday gift. So when Anne discovered the red-and-white-checked book among her birthday gifts, she was delighted. She promised herself that she would write in the book regularly.

Even though she had several good friends—Lies and Jopie and Sanne—she considered the new diary to be her closest friend. She decided that she would call this new and private friend "Kitty" and that the entries she wrote in the diary would be in the form of letters. She would be able to tell Kitty personal things that she had never shared with her real-life friends or with her mother or her sister. She could write whatever she wished because it was unlikely that anyone else would ever read what she wrote. After all, Anne thought as she began to fill the blank pages of her diary, who would possibly be interested in the words of a thirteen-year-old schoolgirl? The first entry was dated Sunday, June 14, 1942. Anne began by describing her birthday.

Less than a month after Anne's birthday, a postcard arrived at the Frank household. Sixteen-year-old Margot had received the dreaded summons from the Germans. The "call-up" meant that she would be taken away to work in a German factory. Worse still, there was much talk in the Jewish community about the concentration camps, where the Germans were deporting a steadily increasing number of Jews. Since no one ever returned to report on these camps, people could only suspect with dread what it would be like to live in one.

Now that the Germans controlled the country, it was impossible for Jews to escape from Holland. Since Otto Frank knew that he and his family could not leave Holland, he thought of an alternate plan. Rather than risk having his family sent away by the Nazis, he would arrange for them to hide somewhere in Holland. Other Jews he knew had already gone into hiding. It was called "diving."

Although the Germans controlled the country, many native Dutch people did not support them. They did not agree with the anti-Semitism of the Germans and felt great compassion for their Jewish neighbors. Some of these Dutch people helped the Jews by letting them hide in their basements, attics, or barns. Some Dutch families even took Jewish infants and young children into their homes and passed the children off as family members. Not only did these people share their rationed food supplies with the Jews, they also put their own lives at risk. If the Germans were to discover that a Dutch family was sheltering Jews, then that family, too, would be arrested and sent to a concentration camp. Nevertheless, thousands of kindhearted Dutch helped the Jews.

Very early in the morning on July 6, 1942, Anne was awakened. Following her mother's instructions, Anne put on layer after layer of clothing. It was not a cold day. But it was the day the family was going into hiding, and it was too risky to be seen carrying suitcases. Anne wore two undershirts, three pairs of pants, a dress, a skirt, a jacket, a summer coat, two pairs of stockings, sturdy shoes, a woolen cap, and a scarf. She must have looked very fat with all that clothing on as she walked down the street with her parents at 7:30 A.M.

Margot had already left with Miep, a typist who worked for the spice firm that Otto Frank had run. Anne didn't know where Margot and Miep were headed. And Anne didn't know where she was going as she walked with her parents out into the rain, each carrying a school satchel and a shopping bag filled with an odd assortment of possessions. She could not take her cat Moortje, but she knew that Moortje would be adopted by the neighbors without any problem.

As they walked along, Anne's parents confided their plan to their daughter. Although they were diving suddenly because of the call-up that Margot had received, they had been planning for this moment for many months. They would be joined by three other Jews: Mr. and Mrs. Van Daan and their fifteen-year-old son Peter. Mr. Van Daan had worked in Otto Frank's spice business. Amazingly, their hiding place would not be out in the country, but in Amsterdam. And even more amazingly, it would be in the building where Otto Frank had once had his office.

When the Germans occupied Holland, one of their regulations forbade Jews to control their own business. But even though Anne's father was no longer the director of his spice company, he was still closely associated with his former employees. And despite the propaganda against the Jews, these Christian employees remained loyal and devoted to their former boss.

[*Edith Frank*]

Anne and her parents walked all the way, in the summer rain, to the building at 263 Prinsengracht. The house had been constructed in the seventeenth century alongside the canal. Because the price of those early houses was determined by their width, Otto Frank's workplace was an extremely narrow building with steep steps leading to the upper floors. Behind the building facing the canal was a second building. It was connected to the first by an internal passageway. Anne had been here before, and she thought she knew the office and the warehouse where spices and herbs were stored. But when she walked up the familiar steep staircase, she was surprised to discover that a small door led to several additional rooms in the back building.

Who could guess that behind the door were two more floors with a total of four rooms, and an attic floor, too? It was here that the Franks and the Van Daans were going to hide.

This clever scheme to hide in Amsterdam—under the very noses of the Nazis—could not have worked without the assistance of a few of Otto Frank's former employees—two older men, Mr. Kraler and Mr. Koophuis, and the two young women who worked in the office as typists, Miep Van Santen and Elli Vossen.

[*Miep Van Santen*]

For many months, Otto Frank's loyal co-workers had been preparing for the arrival of their Jewish friends. The hidden rooms were filled with dishes, rugs, bedclothes, clothing, books, and furniture. There were boxes of canned food, too. Each item had been brought into the building secretly. Not only did these devoted friends have to be sure that the Germans were unaware of what they were doing, but they had to take care that the other workers at the business did not know either.

Mr. Kraler and Mr. Koophuis felt that it was important to involve as few people as possible in this scheme. The Germans were offering reward money to those who helped them find hidden Jews. So everyone had to be very cautious if the Franks and the Van Daans were going to hide successfully until the enemy was defeated.

The first days in hiding were busy. Because their move had taken place earlier than was originally planned, there was a great deal to be done by all of them. The boxes containing the Franks' possessions, which had been secretly sent ahead, were now waiting to be unpacked. Dark blackout curtains had to be made for all the windows so that no light would guide English and American planes flying overhead. But for the Franks, the curtains served another purpose. No one was to guess that these back rooms at 263 Prinsengracht were occupied. The workday ended at 5:30 P.M. People would become suspicious if they knew that the building was occupied after hours.

The four rooms were divided up. Anne's parents had the larger room, just above the office. Next door was a small, narrow room that Anne and Margot were to share. At first, it looked bare and stark, not at all like their attractive rooms at home. But Otto Frank surprised Anne by showing her that he had packed her collection of picture postcards and magazine cutouts of movie stars. Using a pot of paste, Anne quickly covered the walls with her favorite pictures. Now, when she walked into her room, movie stars like Ginger Rogers, Deanna Durbin, and Greta Garbo were smiling at her. She also pasted up a picture of the Dutch royal family. How good it was to know that they, too, were safe from the Nazis.

There were many rules that Anne and her family had to follow if their hiding place was to remain secret. Although they had a bathroom and a kitchen with running water, during the day the water could not be used. That meant that the toilet could not be flushed and pots of water had to be filled for use during the day. Many people came regularly to the lower floors at 263 Prinsengracht to conduct business. These people must not hear any strange noises overhead. Anne and the others had to tiptoe about in bedroom slippers, talking softly and even smothering their coughs. It was a relief when 5:30 came and it was safe to flush the toilet and to speak out loud once again.

Yet, even at night, the hiders had to restrain themselves. It was quiet in the buildings all around them, and the Franks had to be careful in case their movements created suspicious echoes along the canal. But through the silence, one sound was constant. The Westertoren clock sounded every quarter of an hour. Otto, Edith, and Margot Frank didn't like that chiming at all. But from the start, Anne loved it. When she lay in her narrow bed at night and it was too dark to see her beloved pictures, the chiming of the clock was like a friend to her.

[*The Westertoren*]

A week after the Frank family settled into life in the hidden rooms, they were joined by Mr. and Mrs. Van Daan and their son Peter. Mr. and Mrs. Van Daan occupied the room above that of Anne's parents. This room served as a kitchen and sitting room during the day. At night, beds were lowered from the walls for Mr. and Mrs. Van Daan to sleep in. Peter Van Daan slept in the small room adjoining his parents' room.

Anne had looked forward to the arrival of the Van Daans. She thought it would be loads of fun when they were all together. In her diary, she wrote to Kitty that living in the secret rooms was "like being on vacation in a very peculiar boardinghouse."

At first, it seemed like fun—two families cosily hiding together. They shared a dangerous secret, and together they felt safe in their secret annex. Mr. Van Daan reported on the rumors he had heard after the Franks had disappeared. Some of the neighbors said that the Frank family had managed to flee to Switzerland. Others insisted that they had seen the Franks depart on a pair of bicycles. Still another woman was certain that the entire family had been taken away in a car by the Nazis in the middle of the night.

During the week that the Franks had been in hiding, more Jews than ever before had been arrested and sent away by the Nazis. No wonder the Franks were delighted to be together, safely out of sight of the Germans. The family would wait out the war together. And someday soon the Germans would be defeated and everyone could return home.

In the meantime, Elli Vossen's father, who was also employed by the spice firm, was let in on the secret of the people in the annex. Mr. Vossen was a clever carpenter. He devised a bookcase that was attached to the door leading to their rooms. It perfectly disguised the entrance to their hiding place. Now, certainly, no one could guess that anything was behind there.

The two families ate their meals together, everyone helping in its preparation and in the cleaning-up afterward. It was nice to have another young person around, even though Peter Van Daan, like Margot Frank, was quiet and didn't speak much. He had brought his cat Mouschi to the annex, which proved very useful. Rats had gotten into the stored bags of food in the attic, but Mouschi soon took care of the rodents.

After a while, however, this cosy safety of the annex was not enough. The hiders could not go outside for fresh air or a walk. They had to look at the same walls and the same faces over and over. Their only trips were to the offices below their rooms. They could go there at night after the staff had departed for the day.

Lack of variety in their days made life tiresome and boring. Otto Frank planned a full schedule of studies for the three young people. When the war was over, he did not want them to be behind in their schoolwork. Besides, studying French verbs and doing arithmetic helped pass the time. Elli, from the office below, sent for a correspondence course so the young people could study shorthand. It would be a useful skill for Anne and Margot to have in the future.

Still, the sameness of the day's routine remained boring. Everyone grew tense and easily irritated. Sharp words were often exchanged, and chatterbox Anne discovered that she was, more often than not, the cause of arguments.

Mrs. Van Daan criticized if Anne did not want to eat a large portion of a detested vegetable. Also, when Anne tried to joke and make comments to relieve the unpleasant mood at mealtime, Mrs. Van Daan was not amused. "It's absurd that Anne's so frightfully spoiled," Mrs. Van Daan said frequently. "I wouldn't put up with it if Anne were my daughter."

Anne was thankful that she was not Mrs. Van Daan's daughter, but her own mother and sister often found fault with her behavior, too. She discovered that it was not easy to be thirteen while being locked away in a hiding place with others who seemed old and serious and unsympathetic so much of the time. Luckily, Anne had her diary.

Even if no one else could understand how she felt and why she acted the way she did, at least Kitty never scolded her. So day after day, when her studies were completed and her chores were done, Anne would find herself a private corner and would tell Kitty what had been occurring in the secret annex.

In November 1942, after the Franks and the Van Daans had been in hiding for four months, it was decided that there was enough room and food in the annex to hide one more person. Mr. Koophuis and Mr. Kraler both agreed that it was "just as dangerous for seven as for eight" to be hidden in the building. A conference was held, and several Jewish friends were considered. It was not easy to select just one individual. Finally, Miep carried a message to Albert Dussel, a dentist whom both families knew.

[*Albert Dussel*]

Dussel arrived and moved his possessions into Anne's small room. He would share it with Anne, and Margot would sleep with her parents. While the eight occupants of the secret annex sat around the table drinking coffee, Dussel told them all that had been happening in Amsterdam during the months they were in hiding. It was news that Miep and their other guardians had avoided speaking of so as not to distress their Jewish friends.

Dussel said that night after night, the German police—the Gestapo—had driven about the city ringing doorbells and inquiring if there were Jews present. When Jews were discovered, they were put into trucks and taken off to Westerbork, a big prison camp that had been set up in Holland. There they had their heads shaved and were forced to live under extremely primitive conditions.

When she heard these stories from Dussel, Anne realized that despite the hardships of being confined in such a small hideaway, she was living in paradise compared to those Jews who had not managed to hide from the Nazis. Anne sat down and wrote in her diary. She knew she was very lucky.

THINKING ABOUT IT

[1]

Instead of Albert Dussell, *you* have been chosen to join the Franks and the Van Daans in hiding. How would you get along with the "chatterbox" Anne? What would you do to avoid boredom? Explain.

[2]

You are Anne, writing to Kitty in your new diary. Which events, feelings, and problems will you write about? What will you say? How will you say it?

[3]

You are Mr. Kraler and a partner is Mr. Koophuis. You agree to allow the Franks and Van Daans to hide in 263 Prinsengracht. To ensure everyone's safety, the two of you must make sure the families follow certain rules. What are they?

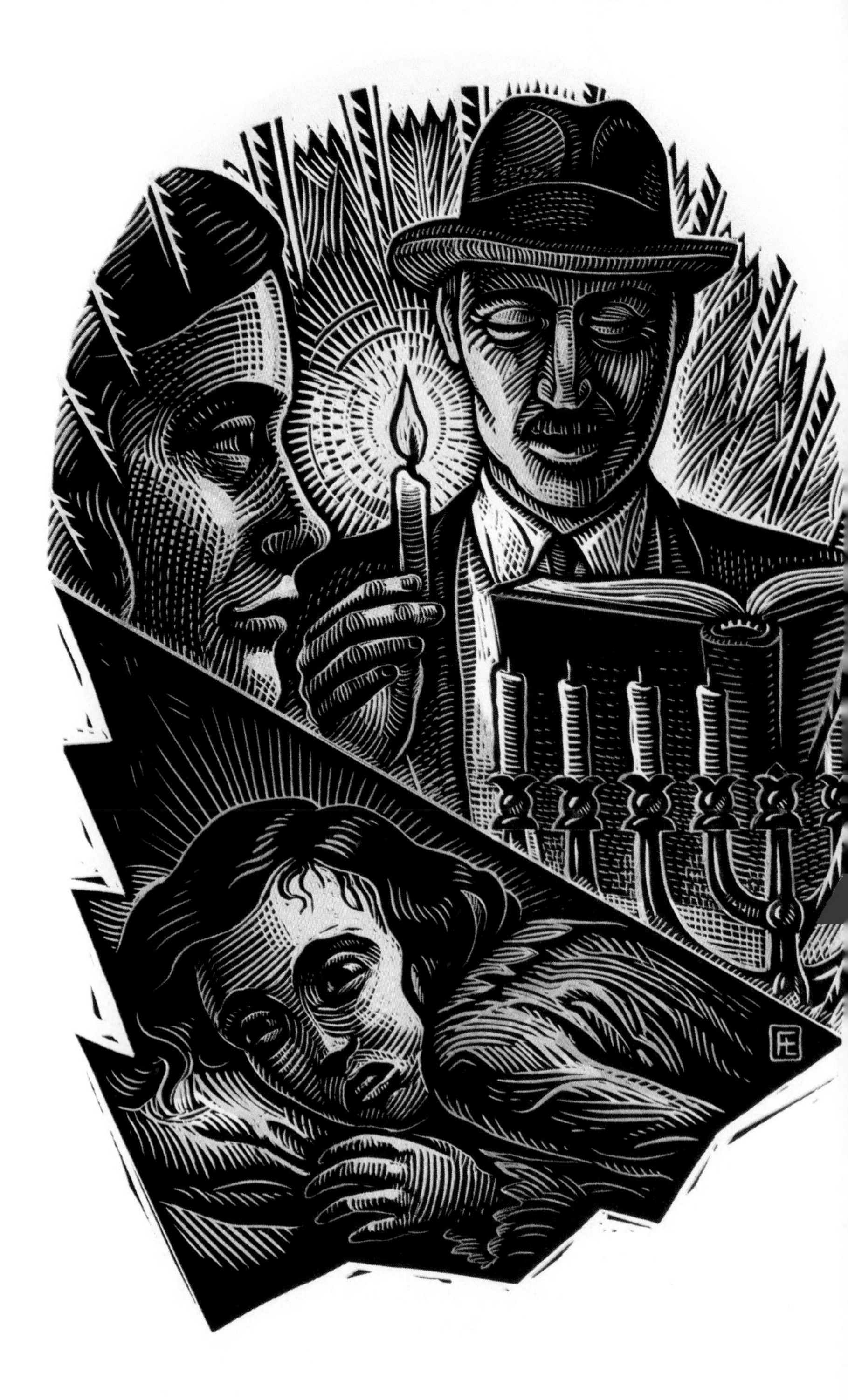

THE DIARY OF ANNE FRANK

by Frances Goodrich

and Albert Hackett

The Diary of Anne Frank
was first presented by Kermit Bloomgarden at
the Cort Theatre, New York City, on October 5, 1955.
It was staged by Garson Kanin,
with setting designed by Boris Aronson.
The cast of characters are:

MR. FRANK	MRS. FRANK
MIEP	MARGOT FRANK
MRS. VAN DAAN	ANNE FRANK
MR. VAN DAAN	MR. KRALER
PETER VAN DAAN	MR. DUSSEL

THE TIME

During the years of World War II

THE PLACE

Amsterdam

[SCENE FOUR]

It is the middle of the night. The stage is dark except for a little light which comes through the skylight in PETER'S *room.*

Everyone is in bed. MR. *and* MRS. FRANK *lie on the couch in the main room, which has been pulled out to serve as a makeshift double bed.*

MARGOT *is sleeping on a mattress on the floor in the main room, behind a curtain stretched across for privacy. The others are all in their accustomed rooms.*

From outside we hear two drunken soldiers singing "Lili Marlene." *A girl's high giggle is heard. The sound of running feet is heard coming closer and then fading in the distance. Throughout the scene there is the distant sound of airplanes passing overhead.*

A match suddenly flares up in the attic. We dimly see MR. VAN DAAN. *He is getting his bearings. He comes quickly down the stairs, and goes to the cupboard where the food is stored. Again the match flares up, and is as quickly blown out. The dim figure is seen to steal back up the stairs.*

There is quiet for a second or two, broken only by the sound of airplanes, and running feet on the street below.

Suddenly, out of the silence and the dark, we hear ANNE *scream.*

ANNE (*screaming*). No! No! Don't . . . don't take me!

(She moans, tossing and crying in her sleep. The other people wake, terrified. DUSSEL *sits up in bed, furious.)*

DUSSEL. Shush! Anne! Anne, for God's sake, shush!

ANNE (*still in her nightmare*). Save me! Save me!

(She screams and screams. DUSSEL *gets out of bed, going over to her, trying to wake her.)*

DUSSEL. For God's sake! Quiet! Quiet! You want someone to hear?

(*In the main room* MRS. FRANK *grabs a shawl and pulls it around her. She rushes in to* ANNE, *taking her in her arms.* MR. FRANK *hurriedly gets up, putting on his overcoat.* MARGOT *sits up, terrified.* PETER'S *light goes on in his room.*)

MRS. FRANK (*to* ANNE, *in her room*). Hush, darling, hush. It's all right. It's all right. (*Over her shoulder to* DUSSEL.) Will you be kind enough to turn on the light, Mr. Dussel? (*Back to* ANNE.) It's nothing, my darling. It was just a dream.

(DUSSEL *turns on the light in the bedroom.* MRS. FRANK *holds* ANNE *in her arms. Gradually* ANNE *comes out of her nightmare, still trembling with horror.* MR. FRANK *comes into the room, and goes quickly to the window, looking out to be sure that no one outside has heard* ANNE'S *screams.* MRS. FRANK *holds* ANNE, *talking softly to her. In the main room* MARGOT *stands on a chair, turning on the center hanging lamp. A light goes on in the* VAN DAANS' *room overhead.* PETER *puts his robe on, coming out of his room.*)

DUSSEL (*to* MRS. FRANK, *blowing his nose*). Something must be done about that child, Mrs. Frank. Yelling like that! Who knows but there's somebody on the streets? She's endangering all our lives.

MRS. FRANK. Anne, darling.

DUSSEL. Every night she twists and turns. I don't sleep. I spend half my night shushing her. And now it's nightmares!

(MARGOT *comes to the door of* ANNE'S *room, followed by* PETER. MR. FRANK *goes to them, indicating that everything is all right.* PETER *takes* MARGOT *back.*)

MRS. FRANK (*to* ANNE). You're here, safe, you see? Nothing has happened. (*To* DUSSEL.) Please, Mr. Dussel, go back to bed. She'll be herself in a minute or two. Won't you, Anne?

DUSSELL *(picking up a book and a pillow)*. Thank you,

but I'm going to the w.c. The one place where there's peace! *(He stalks out.* MR. VAN DAAN*, in underwear and trousers, comes down the stairs.)*

MR. VAN DAAN (*to* DUSSEL). What is it? What happened?

DUSSEL. A nightmare. She was having a nightmare!

MR. VAN DAAN. I thought someone was murdering her.

DUSSEL. Unfortunately, no. (*He goes into the bathroom.* MR. VAN DAAN *goes back up the stairs.* MR. FRANK, *in the main room, sends* PETER *back to his own bedroom.*)

MR. FRANK. Thank you, Peter. Go back go bed. (PETER *goes back to his room.* MR. FRANK *follows him, turning out the light and looking out the window. Then he goes back to the main room, and gets up on a chair, turning out the center hanging lamp.*)

MRS. FRANK (*to* ANNE). Would you like some water? (ANNE *shakes her head.*) Was it a very bad dream? Perhaps if you told me . . . ?

ANNE. I'd rather not talk about it.

MRS. FRANK. Poor darling. Try to sleep then. I'll sit right here beside you until you fall asleep. (*She brings a stool over, sitting there.*)

ANNE. You don't have to.

MRS. FRANK. But I'd like to stay with you . . . very much. Really.

ANNE. I'd rather you didn't.

MRS. FRANK. Good night, then. (*She leans down to kiss* ANNE. ANNE *throws her arm up over her face, turning away.* MRS. FRANK, *hiding her hurt, kisses* ANNE'S *arm.*) You'll be all right? There's nothing that you want?

ANNE. Will you please ask Father to come.

MRS. FRANK (*after a second*). Of course, Anne dear. (*She hurries out into the other room.* MR. FRANK *comes to her as she comes in.*) *Sie verlangt nach Dir!*[1]

[1] *Sie verlangt nach Dir!* She wants to see you.

MR. FRANK (*sensing her hurt*). Edith, *Liebe, schau . . .*[2]

MRS. FRANK. *Es macht nichts! Ich danke dem lieben Herrgott, dass sie sich wenigstens an Dich wendet, wenn sie Trost braucht! Geh hinein, Otto, sie ist ganz hysterisch vor Angst.*[3] (*As* MR. FRANK *hesitates.*) *Geh zu ihr.*[4] (*He looks at her for a second and then goes to get a cup of water for* ANNE. MRS. FRANK *sinks down on the bed, her face in her hands, trying to keep from sobbing aloud.* MARGOT *comes over to her, putting her arms around her.*) She wants nothing of me. She pulled away when I leaned down to kiss her.

MARGOT. It's a phase . . . You heard Father . . . Most girls go through it . . . they turn to their fathers at this age . . . they give all their love to their fathers.

MRS. FRANK. You weren't like this. You didn't shut me out.

MARGOT. She'll get over it . . . (*She smooths the bed for* MRS. FRANK *and sits beside her a moment as* MRS. FRANK *lies down. In* ANNE'S *room* MR. FRANK *comes in, sitting down by* ANNE. ANNE *flings her arms around him, clinging to him. In the distance we hear the sound of ack-ack.*)

ANNE. Oh, Pim. I dreamed that they came to get us! The Green Police! They broke down the door and grabbed me and started to drag me out the way they did Jopie.[5]

MR. FRANK. I want you to take this pill.

ANNE. What is it?

MR. FRANK. Something to quiet you. (*She takes it and drinks the water. In the main room* MARGOT *turns*

[2] *Edith, Liebe, schau . . .* Edith, my dear, look . . .

[3] *Es macht nichts! . . . vor Angst.* It doesn't matter. Thank God that she at least turns to you when she is in need of consolation. Go, Otto, she is hysterical with fear.

[4] *Geh zu ihr.* Go to her.

[5] Anne's best friend who was captured and sent to a concentration camp

out the light and goes back to her bed.)

MR. FRANK (*to* ANNE). Do you want me to read to you for a while?

ANNE. No. Just sit with me for a minute. Was I awful? Did I yell terribly loud? Do you think anyone outside could have heard?

MR. FRANK. No. No. Lie quietly now. Try to sleep.

ANNE. I'm a terrible coward. I'm so disappointed in myself. I think I've conquered my fear . . . I think I'm really grown-up . . . and then something happens . . . and I run to you like a baby . . . I love you, Father. I don't love anyone but you.

MR. FRANK (*reproachfully*). Annele!

ANNE. It's true. I've been thinking about it for a long time. You're the only one I love.

MR. FRANK. It's fine to hear you tell me that you love me. But I'd be happier if you said you loved your mother as well . . . She needs your help so much . . . your love . . .

ANNE. We have nothing in common. She doesn't understand me. Whenever I try to explain my views on life to her she asks me if I'm constipated.

MR. FRANK. You hurt her very much now. She's crying. She's in there crying.

ANNE. I can't help it. I only told the truth. I didn't want her here . . . (*Then, with sudden change.*) Oh, Pim, I was horrible, wasn't I? And the worst of it is, I can stand off and look at myself doing it and know it's cruel and yet I can't stop doing it. What's the matter with me? Tell me. Don't say it's just a phase! Help me.

MR. FRANK. There is so little that we parents can do to help our children. We can only try to set a good example . . . point the way. The rest you must do yourself. You must build your own character.

ANNE. I'm trying. Really I am. Every night I think back over all of the things I did that day that were wrong . . . like putting the wet mop in Mr. Dussel's bed . . . and this thing now with Mother. I say to myself, that was wrong. I make up my mind, I'm never going to do that again. Never! Of course I may do something worse . . . but at least I'll never do *that* again! . . . I have a nicer side, Father . . . a sweeter, nicer side. But I'm scared to show it. I'm afraid that people are going to laugh at me if I'm serious. So the mean Anne comes to the outside and the good Anne stays on the inside, and I keep on trying to switch them around and have the good Anne outside and the bad Anne inside and be what I'd like to be . . . and might be . . . if only . . . only . . .

(*She is asleep.* MR. FRANK *watches her for a moment and then turns off the light, and starts out. The lights dim out. The curtain falls on the scene.* ANNE'S VOICE *is heard dimly at first, and then with growing strength.*)

ANNE'S VOICE. . . . The air raids are getting worse. They come over day and night. The noise is terrifying. Pim says it should be music to our ears. The more planes, the sooner will come the end of the war. Mrs. Van Daan pretends to be a fatalist. What will be, will be. But when the planes come over, who is the most frightened? No one else but Petronella! . . . Monday, the ninth of November, nineteen forty-two. Wonderful news! The Allies have landed in Africa. Pim says that we can look for an early finish to the war. Just for fun he asked each of us what was the first thing we wanted to do when we got out of here. Mrs. Van Daan longs to be home with her own things, her needle-point chairs, the Beckstein piano her father gave her . . . the best that money could buy. Peter would like to go to a movie. Mr. Dussel wants to get back to his dentist's drill. He's afraid he is losing his touch. For myself, there are so many things . . . to ride a bike again . . . to laugh till my belly aches . . . to have new clothes from the skin out . . . to have a hot tub filled to overflowing and wallow in it for hours . . . to be back in school with my friends . . .

(*As the last lines are being said, the curtain rises on the scene. The lights dim on as* ANNE'S VOICE *fades away.*)

[SCENE FIVE]

It is the first night of the Hanukkah celebration. MR. FRANK *is standing at the head of the table on which is the Menorah. He lights the Shamos, or servant candle, and holds it as he says the blessing. Seated listening is all of the "family," dressed in their best. The men wear hats,* PETER *wears his cap.*

MR. FRANK (*reading from a prayer book*). "Praised be Thou, oh Lord our God, Ruler of the universe, who has sanctified us with Thy commandments and bidden us kindle the Hanukkah lights. Praised be Thou, oh Lord our God, Ruler of the universe, who has wrought wondrous deliverances for our fathers in days of old. Praised be Thou, oh Lord our God, Ruler of the universe, that Thou has given us life and sustenance and brought us to this happy season." (MR. FRANK *lights the one candle of the Menorah as he continues.*) "We kindle this Hanukkah light to celebrate the great and wonderful deeds wrought through the zeal with which God filled the hearts of the heroic Maccabees, two thousand years ago. They fought against indifference, against tyranny and oppression, and they restored our Temple to us. May these lights remind us that we should ever look to God, whence cometh our help." Amen. [Pronounced O-mayn.]

ALL. Amen.

(MR. FRANK *hands* MRS. FRANK *the prayer book.*)

MRS. FRANK (*reading*). "I lift up mine eyes unto the mountains, from whence cometh my help. My help cometh from the Lord who made heaven and earth. He will not suffer thy foot to be moved. He that keepeth thee will not slumber. He that keepeth Israel doth neither slumber nor sleep. The Lord is thy keeper. The Lord is thy shade upon thy right hand. The sun shall not smite thee by day, nor the moon by night. The Lord shall keep thee from all evil. He shall keep thy soul. The Lord shall guard thy going out and thy coming in, from this time forth and forevermore." Amen.

ALL. Amen.

(MRS. FRANK *puts down the prayer book and goes to get the food and wine.* MARGOT *helps her.* MR. FRANK *takes the men's hats and puts them aside.*)

DUSSEL (*rising*). That was very moving.

ANNE (*pulling him back*). It isn't over yet!

MRS. VAN DAAN. Sit down! Sit down!

ANNE. There's a lot more, songs and presents.

DUSSEL. Presents?

MRS. FRANK. Not this year, unfortunately.

MRS. VAN DAAN. But always on Hanukkah everyone gives presents . . . everyone!

DUSSEL. Like our St. Nicholas' Day.

(*There is a chorus of "no's" from the group.*)

MRS. VAN DAAN. No! Not like St. Nicholas! What kind of a Jew are you that you don't know Hanukkah?

MRS. FRANK (*as she brings the food*). I remember particularly the candles . . . First one, as we have tonight. Then the second night you light two candles, the next night three . . . and so on until you have eight candles burning. When there are eight candles it is truly beautiful.

MRS. VAN DAAN. And the potato pancakes.

MR. VAN DAAN. Don't talk about them!

MRS. VAN DAAN. I make the best *latkes* you ever tasted!

MRS. FRANK. Invite us all next year . . . in your own home.

MR. FRANK. God willing!

MRS. VAN DAAN. God willing.

MARGOT. What I remember best is the presents we used to get when we were little . . . eight days of presents . . . and each day they got better and better.

MRS. FRANK (*sitting down*). We are all here, alive. That is present enough.

ANNE. No, it isn't. I've got something . . . (*She rushes into her room, hurriedly puts on a little hat improvised from the lamp shade, grabs a satchel bulging with parcels and comes running back.*)

MRS. FRANK. What is it?

ANNE. Presents!

MRS. VAN DAAN. Presents!

DUSSEL. Look!

MRS. VAN DAAN. What's she got on her head?

PETER. A lamp shade!

ANNE (*she picks out one at random*). This is for Margot. (*She hands it to* MARGOT, *pulling her to her feet.*) Read it out loud.

MARGOT (*reading*).

"You have never lost your temper.
You never will, I fear,
You are so good.
But if you should,
Put all your cross words here."

(*She tears open the package.*) A new crossword puzzle book! Where did you get it?

ANNE. It isn't new. It's one that you've done. But I rubbed it all out, and if you wait a little and forget, you can do it all over again.

MARGOT (*sitting*). It's wonderful, Anne. Thank you. You'd never know it wasn't new.

(*From outside we hear the sound of a streetcar passing.*)

ANNE (*with another gift*). Mrs. Van Daan.

MRS. VAN DAAN (*taking it*). This is awful . . . I haven't anything for anyone . . . I never thought . . .

MR. FRANK. This is all Anne's idea.

MRS. VAN DAAN (*holding up a bottle*). What is it?

ANNE. It's hair shampoo. I took all the odds and ends of soap and mixed them with the last of my toilet water.

MRS. VAN DAAN. Oh, Anneke!

ANNE. I wanted to write a poem for all of them, but I didn't have time. (*Offering a large box to* MR. VAN DAAN.) Yours, Mr. Van Daan, is *really* something . . . something you want more than anything. (*As she waits for him to open it.*) Look! Cigarettes!

MR. VAN DAAN. Cigarettes!

ANNE. Two of them! Pim found some old pipe tobacco in the pocket lining of his coat . . . and we made them . . . or rather, Pim did.

MRS. VAN DAAN. Let me see . . . Well, look at that! Light it, Putti! Light it.

(MR. VAN DAAN *hesitates.*)

ANNE. It's tobacco, really it is! There's a little fluff in it, but not much.

(*Everyone watches as* MR. VAN DAAN *cautiously lights it. The cigarette flares up. Everyone laughs.*)

PETER. It works!

MRS. VAN DAAN. Look at him.

MR. VAN DAAN (*spluttering*). Thank you, Anne. Thank you.

(ANNE *rushes back to her satchel for another present.*)

ANNE (*handing her mother a piece of paper*). For Mother, Hanukkah greeting. (*She pulls her mother to her feet.*)

MRS. FRANK (*She reads*). "Here's an I.O.U. that I promise to pay.
Ten hours of doing whatever you say.
Signed, Anne Frank." (MRS. FRANK, *touched, takes* ANNE *in her arms, holding her close.*)

DUSSEL (*to* ANNE). Ten hours of doing what you're told? *Anything* you're told?

ANNE. That's right.

DUSSEL. You wouldn't want to sell that, Mrs. Frank?

MRS. FRANK. Never! This is the most precious gift I've ever had! (*She sits, showing her present to the others.* ANNE *hurries back to the satchel and pulls out a scarf.*)

ANNE (*offering it to her father*). For Pim.

MR. FRANK. Anneke . . . I wasn't supposed to have a present! (*He takes it, unfolding it and showing it to the others.*)

ANNE. It's a muffler . . . to put round your neck . . . like an ascot, you know. I made it myself out of odds and ends . . . I knitted it in the dark each night, after I'd gone to bed. I'm afraid it looks better in the dark!

MR. FRANK (*putting it on*). It's fine. It fits me perfectly. Thank you, Annele.

(ANNE *hands* PETER *a ball of paper, with a string attached to it.*)

ANNE. That's for Mouschi.

PETER (*rising to bow*). On behalf of Mouschi, I thank you.

ANNE (*hesistant, handing him a gift*). And . . . this is yours . . . from Mrs. Quack Quack. (*As he holds it gingerly in his hands.*) Well . . . open it . . . Aren't you going to open it?

PETER. I'm scared to. I know something's going to jump out and hit me.

ANNE. No. It's nothing like that, really.

MRS. VAN DAAN (*as he is opening it*). What is it, Peter? Go on. Show it.

ANNE (*excitedly*). It's a safety razor!

DUSSEL. A what?

ANNE. A razor!

MRS. VAN DAAN (*looking at it*). You didn't make that out of odds and ends.

ANNE (*to* PETER). Miep got it for me. It's not new. It's second-hand. But you really do need a razor now.

DUSSEL. For what?

ANNE. Look on his upper lip . . . you can see the beginning of a mustache.

DUSSEL. He wants to get rid of that? Put a little milk on it and let the cat lick it off.

PETER (*starting for his room*). Think you're funny, don't you.

DUSSEL. Look! He can't wait! He's going in to try it!

PETER. I'm going to give Mouschi his present! (*He goes into his room, slamming the door behind him.*)

MR. VAN DAAN (*disgustedly*). Mouschi, Mouschi, Mouschi.

(*In the distance we hear a dog persistently barking.* ANNE *brings a gift to* MR. DUSSEL.)

ANNE. And last but never least, my roommate, Mr. Dussel.

DUSSEL. For me? You have something for me? (*He opens the small box she gives him.*)

ANNE. I made them myself.

DUSSEL (*puzzled*). Capsules! Two capsules!

ANNE. They're ear-plugs!

DUSSEL. Ear-plugs?

ANNE. To put in your ears so you won't hear me when I thrash around at night. I saw them advertised in a magazine. They're not real ones . . . I made them out of cotton and candle wax. Try them . . . See if they don't work . . . see if you can hear me talk . . .

DUSSEL (*putting them in his ears*). Wait now until I get them in . . . so.

ANNE. Are you ready?

DUSSEL. Huh?

ANNE. Are you ready?

DUSSEL. Good God! They've gone inside! I can't get them out! (*They laugh as* MR. DUSSEL *jumps about, trying to shake the plugs out of his ears. Finally he gets them out. Putting them away.*) Thank you, Anne! Thank you!

MR. VAN DAAN. A real Hanukkah!
MRS. VAN DAAN. Wasn't it cute of her?
MRS. FRANK. I don't know when she did it.
MARGOT. I love my present.
} (*Together.*)

ANNE (*sitting at the table*). And now let's have the song, Father . . . please . . . (*To* DUSSEL.) Have you heard the Hanukkah song, Mr. Dussel? The song is the whole thing! (*She sings.*) "Oh, Hanukkah! Oh, Hanukkah! The sweet celebration . . ."

MR. FRANK (*quieting her*). I'm afraid, Anne, we shouldn't sing that song tonight. (*To* DUSSEL.) It's a song of jubilation, of rejoicing. One is apt to become too enthusiastic.

ANNE. Oh, please, please. Let's sing the song. I promise not to shout!

MR. FRANK. Very well. But quietly now . . . I'll keep an eye on you and when . . .

(*As* ANNE *starts to sing, she is interrupted by* DUSSEL *who is snorting and wheezing.*)

DUSSEL (*pointing to* PETER). You . . . You! (PETER *is coming from his bedroom, ostentatiously holding a bulge in his coat as if he were holding his cat, and dangling* ANNE'S *present before it.*) How many times . . . I told you . . . Out! Out!

MR. VAN DAAN (*going to* PETER). What's the matter with you? Haven't you any sense? Get that cat out of here.

PETER (*innocently*). Cat?

MR. VAN DAAN. You heard me. Get it out of here!

PETER. I have no cat. (*Delighted with his joke, he opens his coat and pulls out a bath towel. The group at the table laugh, enjoying the joke.*)

DUSSEL (*still wheezing*). It doesn't need to be the cat . . . his clothes are enough . . . when he comes out of that room . . .

MR. VAN DAAN. Don't worry. You won't be bothered any more. We're getting rid of it.

DUSSEL. At last you listen to me. (*He goes off into his bedroom.*)

MR. VAN DAAN (*calling after him*). I'm not doing it for you. That's all in your mind . . . all of it! (*He starts back to his place at the table.*) I'm doing it because I'm sick of seeing that cat eat all our food.

PETER. That's not true! I only give him bones . . . scraps . . .

MR. VAN DAAN. Don't tell me! He gets fatter every day! Damn cat looks better than any of us. Out he goes tonight!

PETER. No! No!

ANNE. Mr. Van Daan, you can't do that! That's Peter's cat. Peter loves that cat.

MRS. FRANK (*quietly*). Anne.

PETER (*to* MR. VAN DAAN). If he goes, I go.

MR. VAN DAAN. Go! Go!

MRS. VAN DAAN. You're not going and the cat's not going! Now please . . . this is Hanukkah . . . Hanukkah . . . this is the time to celebrate . . . What's the matter with all of you? Come on, Anne. Let's have the song.

ANNE (*singing*).

"Oh, Hanukkah! Oh, Hanukkah!
The sweet celebration."

MR. FRANK (*rising*). I think we should first blow out the candle . . . then we'll have something for to-morrow night.

MARGOT. But, Father, you're supposed to let it burn itself out.

MR. FRANK. I'm sure that God understands shortages. (*Before blowing it out.*) "Praised be Thou, oh Lord our God, who hast sustained us and permitted us to celebrate this joyous festival."

THINKING ABOUT IT

[1]

Anne's nightmare is about being caught by the police. What is your nightmare—one that woke you up? Think about it. Figure out why you had that particular dream.

[2]

Actors and their directors must first see and hear the play in their minds. They find speeches and stage business that give them clues to the drama and ideas for making it fascinating. What clues to acting and directing *The Diary of Anne Frank* do you find as you read this script?

[3]

If you were at the Hanukkah celebration, what gift would Anne make or find for you? What gift would you make or find for Anne? Tell why.

GOOD AT HEART

from

The Diary of a Young Girl

by Anne Frank

[FRIDAY, 23 JULY, 1943]

Dear Kitty,

Just for fun I'm going to tell you each person's first wish, when we are allowed to go outside again. Margot and Mr. Van Daan long more than anything for a hot bath filled to overflowing and want to stay in it for half an hour. Mrs. Van Daan wants most to go and eat cream cakes immediately. Dussel thinks of nothing but seeing

Lotje, his wife; Mummy of her cup of coffee; Daddy is going to visit Mr. Vossen first; Peter the town and a cinema, while I should find it so blissful, I shouldn't know where to start! But most of all, I long for a home of our own, to be able to move freely and to have some help with my work again at last, in other words—school.

Elli has offered to get us some fruit. It costs next to nothing—grapes f.5.00 per kilo, gooseberries f.0.70 per pound, one peach f.0.50, one kilo melon f.1.50. Then you see in the newspapers every evening in bold letters, "Play fair and keep prices down!"

Yours, Anne

[MONDAY EVENING, 8 NOVEMBER, 1943]

Dear Kitty,

If you were to read my pile of letters one after another, you would certainly be struck by the many different moods in which they are written. It annoys me that I am so dependent on the atmosphere here, but I'm certainly not the only one—we all find it the same. If I read a book that impresses me, I have to take myself firmly in hand, before I mix with other people; otherwise they would think my mind rather queer. At the moment, as you've probably noticed, I'm going through a spell of being depressed. I really couldn't tell you why it is, but I believe it's just because I'm a coward, and that's what I keep bumping up against.

This evening, while Elli was still here, there was a long, loud, penetrating ring at the door. I turned white at once, got a tummy-ache and heart palpitations, all from fear. At night, when I'm in bed, I see myself alone in a dungeon, without Mummy and Daddy. Sometimes I wander by the roadside, or our "Secret Annexe" is on fire, or they come and take us away at night. I see everything as if it is actually taking place, and this gives me the feeling that it may all happen to me very soon! Miep often says she envies us for possessing such tranquillity here. That may be true, but she is not thinking about all our fears. I simply can't imagine that the world will ever be normal for us again. I do talk about "after the war," but then it is only a castle in the air, something that will never really happen. If I think back to our old house, my girl friends, the fun at school, it is just as if another person lived it all, not me.

I see the eight of us with our "Secret Annexe" as if

we were a little piece of blue heaven, surrounded by heavy black rain clouds. The round, clearly defined spot where we stand is still safe, but the clouds gather more closely about us and the circle which separates us from the approaching danger closes more and more tightly. Now we are so surrounded by danger and darkness that we bump against each other, as we search desperately for a means of escape. We all look down below, where people are fighting each other, we look above, where it is quiet and beautiful, and meanwhile we are cut off by the great dark mass, which will not let us go upwards, but which stands before us as an impenetrable wall; it tries to crush us, but cannot do so yet. I can only cry and implore: "Oh, if only the black circle could recede and open the way for us!"

Yours, Anne

[SATURDAY, 15 JULY, 1944]

Dear Kitty,

"For in its innermost depths youth is lonelier than old age." I read this saying in some book and I've always remembered it, and found it to be true. Is it true then that

grownups have a more difficult time here than we do? No. I know it isn't. Older people have formed their opinions about everything, and don't waver before they act. It's twice as hard for us young ones to hold our ground, and maintain our opinions, in a time when all ideals are being shattered and destroyed, when people are showing their worst side, and do not know whether to believe in truth and right and God.

Anyone who claims that the older ones have a more difficult time here certainly doesn't realize to what extent our problems weigh down on us, problems for which we are probably much too young, but which thrust themselves upon us continually, until, after a long time, we think we've found a solution, but the solution doesn't seem able to resist the facts which reduce it to nothing again. That's the difficulty in these times: ideals, dreams, and cherished hopes rise within us, only to meet the horrible truth and be shattered.

It's really a wonder that I haven't dropped all my ideals, because they seem so absurd and impossible to carry out. Yet I keep them, because in spite of everything I still believe that people are really good at heart. I simply can't build up my hopes on a foundation consisting of confusion, misery, and death. I see the world gradually being turned into a wilderness, I hear the ever approaching thunder, which will destroy us too, I can feel the sufferings of millions and yet, if I look up into the heavens, I think that it will all come right, that this cruelty too will end, and that peace and tranquillity will return again.

In the meantime, I must uphold my ideals, for perhaps the time will come when I shall be able to carry them out.

Yours, Anne

EPILOGUE

Anne's diary ends on August 1, 1944. On August 4, the Green Police raided the Secret Annex. All the occupants were arrested and sent to concentration camps, ending their twenty-five months of confinement.

At the end of the war, Mr. Frank was the only occupant of the Secret Annex who returned home. He learned that Anne had been sent to Bergen-Belsen, a concentration camp in Germany, where she died alone at the age of fifteen. He also found that Miep and Elli had saved Anne's diary from a pile of papers left on the Annex floor. He was so moved by Anne's words that he later agreed to have her book printed, translated into every major language, recreated into an important drama, and made into a motion picture. His generosity lets us share Anne's spark of life in the midst of the horrors of World War II.

THINKING ABOUT IT

[1]

In her diary, Anne discusses her reactions to the quote, "For in its innermost depths youth is lonelier than old age." Discuss your reaction to the quote.

[2]

You have been reading about Anne Frank—from a biography, a play, and her own diary. Which type of writing tells the most about Anne? What kinds of information do you learn from each type?

[3]

Anne describes the Secret Annex as "a little piece of blue heaven, surrounded by heavy black rain clouds." How would you describe the Annex?

Another Book About Making a Difference

Like Anne Frank, Dawan, in *Sing to the Dawn* by Minfong Ho, believes that goodness and justice will triumph, but in her native Thailand Dawan faces stiff odds, especially from her own family.

Dream Variation

To fling my arms wide
In some place
    of the sun,
To whirl and to dance
Till the white day
    is done.
Then rest at
    cool evening
Beneath a tall tree
While night comes
    on gently,
    Dark like me—
That is my dream!

To fling my arms wide
In the face of the sun,
Dance! Whirl! Whirl!
Till the quick day
    is done.
Rest at pale evening . . .
A tall, slim tree . . .
Night coming tenderly
    Black like me.

Langston Hughes

Dreams

Hold fast to dreams
For if dreams die
Life is a broken-winged
    bird
That cannot fly.

Hold fast to dreams
For when dreams go
Life is a barren field
Frozen with snow.

Langston Hughes

The Dream Keeper

Bring me all
　　of your dreams,
You dreamers,
Bring me all of your
Heart melodies
That I may wrap them
In a blue cloud cloth
Away from
　　the too-rough fingers
Of the world.

Langston Hughes

Harlem

What happens
　　to a dream deferred?

Does it dry up
like a raisin in the sun?
Or fester like a sore—
And then run?
Does it stink
　　like rotten meat?
Or crust and
　　sugar over—
like a syrupy sweet?

Maybe it just sags
like a heavy load.

　　Or does it explode?

Langston Hughes

During the winter of 1837–38, the Canadian Blackfoot people were hit with a smallpox epidemic. While Shabby-Bull goes to check on other members of his people, his daughter Sweetgrass is left to care for her ill mother and brother, Almost-Mother and Otter.

The River Demon

from Sweetgrass *by Jan Hudson*

There was no food for Otter and there was nobody to get any except me. All I wanted to do was sit and go into a fire trance like Almost-Mother had done.

Our babies were dead. But if I surrendered to my lazy desire, we all would die of hunger. People coming out of sickness especially need food.

"I will find something, Otter. Everything will be all right."

Father had taken the only working rifle, leaving an old musket. No one had fired it for years. It was a flintlock like our rifle, but it used a much larger and wilder bullet. A man of my tribe once killed his close friend with a gun like that, aiming at a buffalo only a spear's length away. I saw it.

A bow and some arrows would be better, if I knew how to handle them. But then I did not know how to creep inside arrow range of an animal, either. The two skills have to go together. Using the musket was necessary.

"What do you do to this gun so it works?" I asked Otter.

My brother watched me, his eyes sparkling against his still-pale face. "You will kill yourself. Better not to ask!" He laughed and leaned back on his sleeping couch.

I did not know whether to be angry because he was teasing me or happy because he laughed. "Just tell me where the big bullets are, Hungry-Otter."

"My sister, you can stop looking. There are none."

No big bullets?

"I melted them all down to use in that rifle Father gave me."

"Aiii, Otter! How am I to feed you?"

Almost-Mother would soon need to eat, too. She had been sleeping more quietly each day that passed.

Luckily there is always gathering—the woman's way of getting food. Somewhere out there, there must be some food for us. Though where, I did not know. I picked up Otter's Hudson's Bay blanket, my woven basket and digging stick, and left.

The sun shone down through a watery sky. The air was a bit cold, but quiet. In fact, the forest was one unearthly silence, broken only by my moccasins drumming out my stride atop an icy crust of snow. Walk carefully, I thought, or you will crash through and cut your ankles. The group of poplars sheltering our tipi probably had wild roses blooming under them last summer.

I was right! Tips of several thorny branches poked through the snow. I dug down, and here and there hid withered rose hips. Thawed, the hips would be furry seeds and mushy fruit inside a brittle and tasteless skin. This meal would scratch all the way down your throat, but was welcome, so very welcome!

I gathered twigs and new little shoots from the younger trees. Many types of these boil into good, filling teas, although they are very bitter. Last I went down to the river, carrying my digging stick.

Along the widest banks were brown spikes of bulrushes as tall as a deer. Somewhere under each one were very tasty roots. But I soon found that river mud freezes as hard as rock. My digging stick only chipped the ground until it finally splintered in two.

All I got was one pale chunk of bulrush root. It looked more like a dirty icicle, certainly not much to carry home to my family.

On my way back, I spied a large white rabbit atop a hill across the river from our camp. My mouth watered as we locked eyes. But my hunger dreams were interrupted.

I heard a spooky noise, one that was new and wrong. Someone was crying inside our tipi. A woman's voice wailed out: it was Almost-Mother, sounding exactly like a woman in deep mourning.

I ran. The basket's high edge hit against my breasts with every footfall. My worst thoughts made me prickle with sweat.

I pushed everything through the tipi flap and dragged myself after.

"Almost-Mother? What is it?" Otter seemed all right.

She had not made any sound for days. She said nothing when our baby died, and did not even blink when I told her Little-Brother was gone too.

"Sweetgrass . . . Otter . . . aiii! My life, all my children," she wailed.

"What is it, Mother?"

"I have always done everything properly, your father will tell you so, and nothing, nothing has ever come back to me as I tried to make it be. Otter is dying, is he not?"

"No," I said quickly, and looked toward my almost-brother. His bright eyes met mine. He looked as worried as I felt.

"Aiii!" wailed Almost-Mother. "Is he dying, Sweetgrass?"

"Look for yourself."

"See, Mother," called Otter from his sleeping couch. "I am fine."

"Everything, everything dies," she cried, "and I am going to die and so are you both and nothing of my life has made the way of anything be anything."

I pulled her body to me so that her head rested on my left shoulder and my mouth was full of her rotten smell of pus.

She was as hot to hold as a charcoal stick burning red at the core. Her cheeks shone a deep purple-brown under her stream of tears. Her thin hands fluttered over the pus and scabs of her face, blindly, fearfully, touching.

When she started calling me Shot-With-Metal, her long-dead sister, I realized her mind was not at all right. Her fever must be mounting. Maybe it would break soon or maybe . . . I stroked her hair until she lay back down. Then I washed her gently, all over.

What a sickness. Here was my almost-mother burning up while her son in the next bed was shaking under mounds of blankets and robes. Now I know what Grandmother meant when she said with smallpox there is no sleep between ice and fire.

Was she dying? I rocked her gently

and pushed away the thought. Her skin had blistered lightly, not close together, and the blisters were small. I felt strange, mothering our tiny mother. But then, was I not a full-grown woman and had she not taken care of me many times when I was sick?

"Is she all right?" asked Otter.

"Yes."

"Good." Pause. "Did you find anything for us to eat?"

The rose hips and the bulrush root made a few spoonfuls of stew. Otter ate most of it. I took some in the big carved-horn spoon Father had made and teased Almost-Mother into swallowing it. There was none left for me.

That was not important, because healthy people can live without food for many days. But I had to get food for my family—good food, enough, and soon. Otherwise only I would greet my father if . . . when he returned. I chewed the inside of my lips: the blood was comfort, and the pain sharpened my thoughts.

I needed wire. Father had traded for some this summer. What was left? I searched through his bags and found a piece as long as my arm. Not enough, but it must do.

Outside, the wind blew softly. If it were a little warmer, the rabbits would wake and run. I slid my fingers down the chilly length of wire and began looking for a rabbit path. On top of the frozen stream were scattered little round scats, and some small trees nearby were nipped at a sharp-pointed angle. Ah, that soft groove worn in the snow down in the bushes. There I would set my snare.

My hands were already whitening, but I thought only of that rabbit I had seen earlier. I tied a loop in the length of wire, then fumbled its free end around the nearest poplar sapling. Finally I arranged the loop to hover over the little trail.

This is how it works. The rabbit comes hopping along his path. He does not understand what that wire is doing and is not too worried. He hops and his head goes through the loop but his shoulders hit the wire. When he panics, the loop tightens around his furry neck, and he struggles harder and harder until it cuts off his air. The rabbit dies. Then he goes home for our stewpot.

That is a painful way to go. Sorry, rabbit, but you have to die for us to live, just as shoots and grasses earlier died for you to live. So it has always been for grasses, rabbits, and my people. In this pattern is comfort.

So I thought as I dragged my weary body home to bed.

My mind surfaced lazily from its cool numb dream. Someone wanted me to do something. Again. Probably something I could not do.

"What is it?"

One day blurred into the next. The mists of morning filled our tipi. Those big begging eyes looked like Little-Brother's. It could not be. They were Otter's eyes. Otter would not beg. But I knew how hunger twists inside and drives you to things you think you would never do.

Some scabs had fallen from my brother's face last night, leaving ugly pits in the skin. Who else would be pitted the next time I saw them? Inside me a deep voice answered: the lucky ones would be pitted. The others I would never see again.

"Sweetgrass? Are you awake?"

"I am now. What do you want?"

"Do you feel Mother is going to die? Am I going to die?"

I hesitated. "No, I do not feel it."

"Are you sure?"

"Pretty well. All the signs look good."

"But Mother is still burning inside."

"True, but you have both lived many days. Grandmother said that with smallpox most of our people die right away. They die and swell up like the baby." I tried to force a laugh through my tight throat. "Do you think I would stay here if you were dying?"

Otter smiled in a way I had never seen before. The softness around his eyes had nothing to do with smallpox.

"If I live, I will give you anything you want."

"Just be my good brother Otter."

He gave me his hand and I held it between mine in my lap.

"I tried to go hunting this morning," he said after a while.

"Otter!"

"You were asleep. Why not go?" he said.

"You are still too weak."

"I almost did not get out of the tipi to relieve myself. You must have been doing some dirty nursing work these last days," he said, grinning unevenly.

I chose not to tell him about the buffalo robes. When their stink became too bad I threw the old sleeping-robes outside and rolled Otter and Almost-Mother onto ones I had been making ready for Father. So no one needed to feel any shame.

"Next hunt, Sweetgrass, every second buffalo hide is yours." He knew.

"I feel I must get well now, sister. Tomorrow I will try again to go hunting."

"Your spirit is rising, but it is still tender. Just rest."

Otter would not hear me. "I can hunt with the bow and arrow and you cannot."

"Just rest."

At long last he relaxed. Luckily he was still too weak to do more than talk.

"So you must not be sad," he continued. "I wanted you to hear me, not to worry, you know, if you . . ."

If I got the smallpox.

I patted his hand and tucked him in. Otter was right. We had better be ready for the sickness coming to me, also. But he was wrong to think he could hunt tomorrow morning, or even the following morning. He must rest for many days, and most of all, if he was to care for us as I had done, he must eat well.

As I put on my mittens and prepared to go out, I thought: Why was the pox so slow coming to me? Most of the time I never thought of getting it. Me die? I would make Otter ready for it, but never would I give in! I would find power to live. *Ahksi kiwa!* My heart sang with the warriors.

I fear nothing!

There was a ghostly world lying between our tipi and my rabbit snare. The night before, Chinook, the warm mountain wind, had melted each tree's robe of snow and then blew fast away to the south. Set free for a moment, the snow-water froze again as ice. Each tree, each twig and bud wore a shining shield that the arrows of the sun bounced off, so dazzling my eyes that there seemed to be no skeletons beneath their bright flesh. This was a spirit world—a world of clearest shadows, the shadows of light.

Ax in hand, I shuffled over the icy surface crust, feeling myself the only creature in this world. Where was the flashing silver of my snare? In the snow's light, it would be hard to see, but I knew exactly where I had placed it. Right beneath those bushes bordering the stream.

The snare was empty! My heart jerked in disbelief at the sight. I shut my eyes and wished it full with a fat, white mound of rabbit.

I had to sit down. For the first time since Father left, I felt sick, really sick. A dizziness had caught me and left me weaker than I had ever been before. I had no choice but to lie back on a shiny crest of ice and let come whatever was in store.

Overhead the sun hummed down from a pale blue sky. I lost myself in the vastness of it all. The world behind me could have vanished for all I knew.

A raven's laugh brought me back. The sun had wandered on, and a light blanket of cloud overcast the sky. It was getting colder.

I took off my mitten and felt my face for spots. There were none. One small relief.

But what could I do? I could not go back without food.

And there were those hungry horses to feed as well. Frustrated, I took up our big ax and swung hard at the last unstripped poplar on this side of the stream. I cut its bark off in rings. As I pulled the inside bark from the rings like I had so often done before, I realized how weak I was fast becoming.

I threw down what strips I had gathered and picked up our bright ax. I might not have much time, I heard myself say.

I headed toward where Otter had hobbled the mares and stallions in the woods behind our tipi, inside the little meadow.

Stumbling through the fringing trees, I seemed to be in a dream where I knew what I had to do. I had to find the horses. We were starving. Horses. Meat. In this dream, the scattered tree stumps were helping me. All the tall ones were Father and the short ones were Little-Brother. But the dark figures changed back into stumps when I looked straight at them. Visions come easy when a person is sick and hungry.

Move carefully now. I must not startle the horses. Into the bitter cold of my nose and mouth crept a faint, foul odor.

Something was wrong.

From my narrow edge of the meadow there were no standing shapes to be seen, except one gray faraway blur against the trees opposite. Maybe it was Otter's stallion. Everything wavered in front of me. Where were our other horses?

A stench rode on the wind twisting through the poplars. I had to spit a lot because it made me gag. And it got worse as I went on. In the snowy meadow, I came upon a heap of gray skin and long ragged bones, which once had been Otter's horse. A leather thong still hobbled what was left of one foreleg. Aiii, the wolves had been hungry, too. The unhobbled ones must have run off.

There was no eating here.

My family's ill luck had now fully ripened. There was nothing here for me to do.

I turned on my heel and hauled my clean ax home.

I chopped and boiled old pemmican sacks for soup while Otter rested on his elbow watching me. Almost-Mother was enjoying a much quieter sleep for the first time. She was getting better, but when she awoke she would need good food. This sack soup tasted of meat and grease, but it was pretty thin. If Otter did not like it, he kept his comments to himself.

"What are we going to do?" he asked after he had eaten his share.

"There are many more pemmican sacks."

"Not enough. Have you thought about the dogs?"

"They left long ago. And the wolves beat us to the horses."

Otter's flushed skin darkened further. We sat silent together awhile, listening to our mother moaning from time to time.

"I will check my snare tomorrow morning."

On the twenty-third morning after Father left us, Almost-Mother's blisters had hardened to scabs. I held her graying head on my lap and spooned pemmican-sack soup into her. She swallowed the watery broth greedily.

For the first time, she turned her face so that her eyes could look into mine. She smiled weakly. Her spirit flickered brighter, like coals being blown on.

Somewhere I would find food for my family.

Out I crept again under the cold dome of the world. Winter was coming back again, full force. Summer seemed only a lying dream to me. I could not shake mocking memories of food eaten for the taste of it, berries thrown on the grass in laughter. I forced my moccasined feet forward. Soon I would be too weak to move them at all. Without smallpox, I might live in this way another moon or longer, hoping for my father's return. But the others would die. Aiii, already I was so lonely.

Was Father alive? Pretty-Girl? Grandmother? Eagle-Sun? The thought of them alive somewhere was a small fire to warm my freezing spirit.

The world was black with shadow, blue-white with sky and snow today—nothing else. The light shimmered off the snow, making my eyes ache. I dragged my ax behind me. If my snare was still empty, there would at least be the untouched poplars on the far side of the stream. If horses ate the green inside bark, then so could we. I found it hard to control my trembling, which came partly from desperation, partly from weakness.

I reached the snare, and its loop was empty. Always empty. So I took it apart.

My damp, mittenless fingers froze to the wire as I unwrapped it from the small tree. By the time I had the snare unsnarled, it was covered with bits of skin and iced with blood. Dragging ax and wire, I trudged up the river.

Under my feet the ice seemed to sway, and sometimes my eyes flooded with a gray fog. I would wait until I got some strength back before I went on. To walk blind on the ice is a good way to die.

Black-Eagle did that once. It was long ago, in the year of the famine. He stepped on a rotten piece of ice, out on one of the rivers in the foothills. His wives never saw Black-Eagle again, not even to bury his body. Here in front of me thrust a big stone. The dark patch on its sunny side was just like the patch Black-Eagle stepped through.

I bent over and stared into that dark ice. It was almost clear, showing water beneath its brittle frozen layers. Something moved in the darkness. With a start, I stepped back a bit. Did the dead seek me to join them?

The movement came again, and I saw it to be a black and narrow slash of a shadow, floating under the ice. As long as my arm at least. It moved sideways again. A river demon's fish!

If I fell through the ice that fish would eat me.

I remembered a story. Sometimes fish were eaten by people. Not by the Blackfoot, but others like the Cree. Our warriors called them fish-eaters in insult.

I had not heard any stories of the Cree being wiped out by river demons.

The ice was very thin here. It felt like a sign to me, the sign I had been seeking.

An evil fish waited under the ice. I would catch him and cook him. I shook with fear and power and loathing. Now.

When I hit the ax on the ice, the demon was

gone like a shot. If he wanted my spirit as much as I wanted his, he would be back.

I chipped with the blade until a bowl-shaped sheet of ice broke out. I swung the ax high and gave the ice underneath a good blow. The metal sunk in sweetly, and the water made a sucking sound when I pulled out the ax. How good to hit something!

I chipped out a big enough hole.

What to do now? I sat on a snowdrift to rest. How do the Cree catch fish?

I shut my eyes and tried to picture, one by one, my dizzy thoughts. Could a fish be grabbed? Not likely with them being so quick and slimy.

Could a fish be shafted upon an ax blade? Maybe. But when my mind pictured it, the fish split, then sank out of sight.

Could a fish be caught like a rabbit in a wire?

I opened my eyes.

I pulled off my mittens again and forced my stiffening fingers to wrap the loose end of the snare around the ax handle. It was hard to get it tight. I cut myself a few times.

The snare must go quietly into the water. I lay down on my belly on the ice.

Down it dipped into the dark hole. Success. The whole loop went all the way under the water. I was afraid I would not have enough wire. I got my mittens back on and prepared myself for a wait.

My plan was to let the fish get his head all the way through before yanking. I had a lot of time to think about it.

I never really noticed before how noisy a quiet forest can be. There is always a bird somewhere calling out to his friends. The wind is always there, rising and falling, talking to every tree. Even the ice groaned.

The ice. At first, it was just cold. Then it hurt. It sent out fingers under my blankets, up and down my spine. I got a little worried when a wash of numbness settled in, but I did not dare move or make a sound.

Then a big pointed head glided into view right under my nose. It stopped short a hand's width from my snare. Dark, cold eyes on the sides of its head could see everywhere. I did not move a muscle.

What now?

I held my breath, and he flicked his fins again. A shivering thought: fish need not follow paths like rabbits do. This creature could swim here or there or even under, and miss my trap!

I knew I had to make my move, but nothing must frighten him. Steady now. I eased the snare over the evil head so gently that it made only an arrowhead ripple where the wire parted the water.

Then the fish shot forward!

I jerked back on the ax handle. I had him!

But how well? Jumping to my feet, I hauled up on the ax handle. The demon thrashed and thumped along on the bottom of the ice before I could get his head free. Then up!

A shower of drops rained down behind him as he landed splat on the ice. His eyes were fierce and he bared a mouthful of terrible tiny teeth. Another flip, a flop, and somehow the fish escaped the wire.

I felt my entire life fall with him in that moment.

The mottled green body arched this way and that. His tail gave the ice mighty slaps, skittering him back toward the hole.

He came to rest on the jagged edge of the icehole, his head only smelling-distance from the open water. I jumped fast to catch him. It was life against life. I sat on top of him, holding his slippery, writhing, slimy body between my legs, and grabbed his gill.

With my other hand, I stretched for the ax, caught the wire, pulled it over. Then I cracked him smartly between the eyes. I gave him another, and another.

I dared not loosen my grip until the fish was truly dead. At last it gave its final spasm, smearing blood and slime all over me and the ice.

Underneath us the river trembled. I froze. It should be a moon or more before the ice broke. Would the river demons take me?

But the air was full of nothing, nothing but a delicious slimy smell. The ice did not crack and the river did not move anymore.

I went home in triumph.

soup cut down its fishy smell. A handful of roots rounded out the taste. Mother drank several spoonfuls that evening and smiled at me again. It was a fine thing to see.

Otter drank some too and even ate flesh from

the pointed bones. He said he was going to vomit. But he did not.

I ate also and went again to the river to catch another fish for my family, the next day and the next. But I went with a buffalo robe to lie on and dried seeds as bait. And I got quite good at brewing tasty broths.

No river demon took me either.

Otter's smallpox scabs fell off day by day. Almost-Mother's blisters dried, and her face filled out and lost its shadow of the death-sign. All because of the fish.

Then came the morning of our twenty-seventh day. While Almost-Mother and Otter were still asleep, I stretched an unfinished hide on the floor and got busy with my rubbing-stone. Now I was strong enough to work some of the unfinished hides to replace the dirty ones I had had to throw out.

A warm Chinook wind spilled down from the mountains that morning and washed across the creek to shake our home. At first I did not worry. Our tipi-pegs were driven deep into the ground. Stones and ice pinned the skirts likewise. I knew we should be safe no matter how hard the wind blew.

It hit the land so fiercely the sound was almost like a creature howling. And there were other spooky noises too—scraping, thuds, and scratchings. I knew it must be dried twigs and branches kicked up against the tipi's front.

It was almost like someone dropping his packs outside, like a shadow-man fumbling at our flap to come in. Someone like a traveler . . . or a spirit.

It could not be. But I heard the sounds happening.

I leaped up and grabbed my friend the ax. There was one last rattle and the triangular flap of our door fell open. Wind gusted around my ankles and filled the tipi. A bending head and a craggy hand reached in. My breath hid scared in my throat. Was that the top-tied hair of a Crow warrior? Or was it . . .

I must stand ready. *Ahksi kiwa!*

Legs, then shoulders, appeared through the tipi flap, and the man straightened himself. Braids lay across his shoulders in the Blackfoot way, not in any other. The face was a face I knew beneath its scarring and death-worn look.

Shabby-Bull, alive, had come home.

Smallpox wounds were pink upon my father's skin. He stood cold-face, making no welcoming sign; his body blocked the wind and the pale dawn light. He stared at the ax in my hand, the two bundled sleepers on the floor, and at the empty place where the finished hides should be.

"Where are the others?" my father asked.

"Otter and Mother are asleep, Father, and the babies are dead." It felt strange to see him, not at all as I expected.

"The babies are dead in Crying-Dog's camp as well. And so are Crying-Dog and his three wives." Father turned and tied the door flap behind him.

I pulled the blankets from the sleeping faces so Father might see them and their healing scars. He stood before them for a moment. Then he told me it was good and I was to pull the blankets up again so no one would wake.

He turned to walk to the man's place at the back of the tipi behind the fire. That limp is bad, I thought, as he dragged his left foot across the floor cover. He stopped by the kettle. Even through the stink of unfinished hides and the smoke of the fire, I could smell the telltale odor of fish. Aiii.

My heart froze, helplessly waiting.

"Daughter, what have you done?"

"We are living, Father," I tried to explain. "Otter and Mother and me, we are living. In Crying-Dog's camp the people are dead."

He glowered at the floor while silence roared between us. Black stubby lashes rimmed my father's dark, unblinking eyes. My mouth tasted salty with blood.

"May you not mourn for this, Sweetgrass."

I knew I would not mourn, ever. My fingernails were cutting into the palms of my hands. I made myself uncurl them.

"Father, I threw out your robes. They were dirty with smallpox."

He was staring at the floor still.

"I tried *hard* to feel which trail to follow," I added, promising myself not to cry. "Father, I am not a warrior!"

"Not a warrior," he repeated, shifting his weight heavily. "But you now are a woman."

Stunned, I looked into his eyes to confirm his words. They were old, much older than when he left, but they were shining clear and proud.

"Come, give an old man a hand to sit down."

I did as he said. His weight on my shoulder, his arm round my waist were sweet indeed.

"I brought you a present. Look outside."

I could hardly see for the tears, but there on the ground by the door lay a freshly killed white rabbit.

In the sky, the sun was climbing.

Thinking About It

1. When you read, you connect your own experience to someone's experience in a story. Tell about that connection as you read "The River Demon."

2. While Sweetgrass has come to visit, a storm blows through your community, causing great destruction. How might Sweetgrass help you and your neighbors?

3. Perhaps no one is really prepared to deal with a crisis. And probably no one should worry all the time about the possibility of disaster. Figure out how to be prepared, yet not worry all the time.

Another Book About Survival

Ann in *Z for Zachariah* by Robert C. O'Brien struggles to survive. As far as she knows, she is the only person left in a world destroyed by nuclear radiation. Then she sees smoke. Will this person be a friend or an enemy?

Brian's parents are divorced, and Brian is on his way to visit his father in northern Canada. When the pilot of the two-seater plane suffers a fatal heart attack and the plane crashes, Brian is forced to survive on his own in the wilderness.

From a Spark

from Hatchet *by Gary Paulsen*

At first he thought it was a growl. In the still darkness of the shelter in the middle of the night his eyes came open and he was awake and he thought there was a growl. But it was the wind, a medium wind in the pines had made some sound that brought him up, brought him awake. He sat up and was hit with the smell.

It terrified him. The smell was one of rot, some musty rot that made him think only of graves with cobwebs and dust and old death. His nostrils widened and he opened his eyes wider but he could see nothing. It was too dark, too hard dark with clouds covering even the small light from the stars, and he could not see. But the smell was alive, alive and full and in the shelter. He thought of the bear, thought of Bigfoot and every monster he had ever seen in every fright movie he had ever watched, and his heart hammered in his throat.

Then he heard the slithering. A brushing sound, a slithering brushing sound near his feet—and he kicked out as hard as he could, kicked out and threw the hatchet at the sound, a noise coming from his throat. But the hatchet missed, sailed into the wall where it hit the rocks with a shower of sparks, and his leg was instantly torn with pain, as if a hundred needles had been driven into it. "Unnnngh!"

Now he screamed, with the pain and fear, and skittered on his backside up into the corner of the shelter, breathing through his mouth, straining to see, to hear.

The slithering moved again, he thought toward him at first, and terror took him, stopping his breath. He felt he could see a low dark form, a bulk in the darkness, a shadow that lived, but now it moved away, slithering and scraping it moved away and he saw or thought he saw it go out of the door opening.

He lay on his side for a moment, then pulled

a rasping breath in and held it, listening for the attacker to return. When it was apparent that the shadow wasn't coming back he felt the calf of his leg, where the pain was centered and spreading to fill the whole leg.

His fingers gingerly touched a group of needles that had been driven through his pants and into the fleshy part of his calf. They were stiff and very sharp on the ends that stuck out, and he knew then what the attacker had been. A porcupine had stumbled into his shelter and when he had kicked it the thing had slapped him with its tail of quills.

He touched each quill carefully. The pain made it seem as if dozens of them had been slammed into his leg, but there were only eight, pinning the cloth against his skin. He leaned back against the wall for a minute. He couldn't leave them in, they had to come out, but just touching them made the pain more intense.

So fast, he thought. So fast things change. When he'd gone to sleep he had satisfaction and in just a moment it was all different. He grasped one of the quills, held his breath, and jerked. It sent pain signals to his brain in tight waves, but he grabbed another, pulled it, then another quill. When he had pulled four of them he stopped for a moment. The pain had gone from being a pointed injury pain to spreading in a hot smear up his leg and it made him catch his breath.

Some of the quills were driven in deeper than others and they tore when they came out. He breathed deeply twice, let half of the breath out, and went back to work. Jerk, pause, jerk—and three more times before he lay back in the darkness, done. The pain filled his leg now, and with it came new waves of self-pity. Sitting alone in the dark, his leg aching, some mosquitos finding him again, he started crying. It was all too much, just too much, and he couldn't take it. Not the way it was.

I can't take it this way, alone with no fire and in the dark, and next time it might be something worse, maybe a bear, and it wouldn't be just quills in the leg, it would be worse. I can't do this, he thought, again and again. I can't. Brian pulled himself up until he was sitting upright back in the corner of the cave. He put his head down on his arms across his knees, with stiffness taking his left leg, and cried until he was cried out.

He did not know how long it took, but later he looked back on this time of crying in the corner of the dark cave and thought of it as when he learned the most important rule of survival, which was that feeling sorry for yourself didn't work. It wasn't just that it was wrong to do, or that it was considered incorrect. It was more than that—it didn't work. When he sat alone in the darkness and cried and was done, was all done with it, nothing had changed. His leg still hurt, it was still dark, he was still alone and the self-pity had accomplished nothing.

At last he slept again, but already his patterns were changing and the sleep was light, a resting doze more than a deep sleep, with small sounds awakening him twice in the rest of the night. In the last doze period before daylight, before he awakened finally with the morning light and the clouds of new mosquitos, he dreamed. This time it was not of his mother, not of the Secret, but of his father at first and then of his friend Terry.

In the initial segment of the dream his father was standing at the side of a living room looking at him and it was clear from his expression that he was trying to tell Brian something. His lips moved but there was no sound, not a whisper. He waved his hands at Brian, made gestures in front of his face as if he were scratching something, and he worked to make a word with his mouth but at first Brian could not see it. Then the lips made an *mmmmm* shape but no sound came. *Mmmmm—maaaa.* Brian could not hear it, could not understand it and he wanted to so badly; it was so important to understand his father, to know what he was saying. He was trying to help, trying so hard, and when Brian couldn't understand he looked cross, the way he did when Brian asked questions more than once, and he faded. Brian's father faded into a fog place Brian could not see and the dream was almost over, or seemed to be, when Terry came.

He was not gesturing to Brian but was sitting in the park at a bench looking at a barbecue pit and for a time nothing happened. Then he got up and poured some charcoal from a bag into the cooker, then some starter fluid, and he took a flick type of lighter and lit the fluid. When it was burning and the charcoal was at last getting hot he turned, noticing Brian for the first time in the dream. He turned and smiled and pointed to the fire as if to say, see, a fire.

But it meant nothing to Brian, except that he wished he had a fire. He saw a grocery sack on the table next to Terry. Brian thought it must contain hot dogs and chips and mustard and he could think only of the food. But Terry shook his head and pointed again to the fire, and twice more he pointed to the fire, made Brian see the flames, and Brian felt his frustration and anger rise and he thought all right, all right, I see the fire but so what? I don't have a fire. I know about fire; I know I need a fire.

I know that.

His eyes opened and there was light in the cave, a gray dim light of morning. He wiped his mouth and tried to move his leg, which had stiffened like wood. There was thirst, and hunger, and he ate some raspberries from the jacket. They had spoiled a bit, seemed softer and mushier, but still had a rich sweetness. He crushed the berries against the roof of his mouth with his tongue and drank the sweet juice as it ran down his throat. A flash of metal caught his eye and he saw his hatchet in the sand where he had thrown it at the porcupine in the dark.

He scootched up, wincing a bit when he bent his stiff leg, and crawled to where the hatchet lay. He picked it up and examined it and saw a chip in the top of the head.

The nick wasn't large, but the hatchet was important to him, was his only tool, and he should not have thrown it. He should keep it in his hand, and make a tool of some kind to help push an animal away. Make a staff, he thought, or a lance, and save the hatchet. Something came then, a thought as he held the hatchet, something about the dream and his father and Terry, but he couldn't pin it down.

"Ahhh . . ." He scrambled out and stood in the morning sun and stretched his back muscles and his sore leg. The hatchet was still in his hand, and as he stretched and raised it over his head it caught the first rays of the morning sun. The first faint light hit the silver of the hatchet and it flashed a brilliant gold in the light. Like fire. That is it, he thought. What they were trying to tell me.

Fire. The hatchet was the key to it all. When he threw the hatchet at the porcupine in the cave and missed and hit the stone wall it had showered sparks, a golden shower of sparks in the dark, as golden with fire as the sun was now.

The hatchet was the answer. That's what his father and Terry had been trying to tell him. Somehow he could get fire from the hatchet. The sparks would make fire.

Brian went back into the shelter and studied the wall. It was some form of chalky granite, or a sandstone, but imbedded in it were large pieces of a darker stone, a harder and darker stone. It only took him a moment to find where the hatchet had struck. The steel had nicked into the edge of one of the darker stone pieces. Brian turned the head backward so he would strike with the flat rear of the hatchet and hit the black rock gently. Too gently, and nothing happened. He struck harder, a glancing blow, and two or three weak sparks skipped off the rock and died immediately.

He swung harder, held the hatchet so it would hit a longer, sliding blow, and the black rock exploded in fire. Sparks flew so heavily that several of them skittered and jumped on the sand beneath the rock and he smiled and struck again and again.

There could be fire here, he thought. I will have a fire here, he thought, and struck again—I will have fire from the hatchet.

Brian found it was a long way from sparks to fire.

Clearly there had to be something for the sparks to ignite, some kind of tinder or kindling—but what? He brought some dried grass in, tapped sparks into it and watched them die. He tried small twigs, breaking them into little pieces, but that was worse than the grass. Then he tried a combination of the two, grass and twigs.

Nothing. He had no trouble getting sparks, but the tiny bits of hot stone or metal—he couldn't tell which they were—just sputtered and died.

He settled back on his haunches in exasperation, looking at the pitiful clump of grass and twigs.

He needed something finer, something soft and fine and fluffy to catch the bits of fire.

Shredded paper would be nice, but he had no paper.

"So close," he said aloud, "so close . . ."

He put the hatchet back in his belt and went out of the shelter, limping on his sore leg. There had to be something, had to be. Man had made fire. There had been fire for thousands, millions of years. There had to be a way.

He dug in his pockets and found the twenty-dollar bill in his wallet. Paper. Worthless paper out here. But if he could get a fire going . . .

He ripped the twenty into tiny pieces, made a pile of pieces, and hit sparks into them. Nothing happened. They just wouldn't take the sparks. But there had to be a way—some way to do it.

Not twenty feet to his right, leaning out over the water were birches and he stood looking at them for a full half-minute before they registered on his mind. They were a beautiful white with bark like clean, slightly speckled paper.

Paper.

He moved to the trees. Where the bark was peeling from the trunks it lifted in tiny tendrils, almost fluffs. Brian plucked some of them loose, rolled them in his fingers. They seemed flammable, dry and nearly powdery. He pulled and twisted bits off the trees, packing them in one hand while he picked them with the other, picking and gathering until he had a wad close to the size of a baseball.

Then he went back into the shelter and arranged the ball of birchbark peelings at the base of the black rock. As an afterthought he threw in the remains of the twenty-dollar bill. He struck and a stream of sparks fell into the bark and quickly died. But this time one spark fell on one small hair of dry bark—almost a thread of bark—and seemed to glow a bit brighter before it died.

The material had to be finer. There had to be a soft and incredibly fine nest for the sparks.

I must make a home for the sparks, he thought. A perfect home or they won't stay, they won't make fire.

He started ripping the bark, using his fingernails at first, and when that didn't work he used the sharp edge of the hatchet, cutting the bark in thin slivers, hairs so fine they were almost not there. It was painstaking work, slow work, and he stayed with it for over two hours. Twice he stopped for a handful of berries and once to go to the lake for a drink. Then back to work, the sun on his back, until at last he had a ball of fluff as big as a grapefruit—dry birchbark fluff.

He positioned his spark nest—as he thought of it—at the base of the rock, used his thumb to make a small depression in the middle, and slammed the back of the hatchet down across the black rock. A cloud of sparks rained down, most of them missing the nest, but some, perhaps thirty or so, hit in the depression and of those six or seven found fuel and grew, smoldered and caused the bark to take on the red glow.

Then they went out.

Close—he was close. He repositioned the nest, made a new and smaller dent with his thumb, and struck again.

More sparks, a slight glow, then nothing.

It's me, he thought. I'm doing something wrong. I do not know this—a cave dweller would have had a fire by now, a Cro-Magnon man would have a fire by now—but I don't know this. I don't know how to make a fire.

Maybe not enough sparks. He settled the nest in place once more and hit the rock with a series of blows, as fast as he could. The sparks poured like a golden waterfall. At first they seemed to take, there were several, many sparks that found life and took briefly, but they all died.

Starved.

He leaned back. They are like me. They are starving. It wasn't quantity, there were plenty of sparks, but they needed more.

I would kill, he thought suddenly, for a book of matches. Just one book. Just one match. I would kill.

What makes fire? He thought back to school. To all those science classes. Had he ever learned what made a fire? Did a teacher ever stand up there and say, "This is what makes a fire . . ."

He shook his head, tried to focus his thoughts. What did it take? You have to have fuel, he thought—and he had that. The bark was fuel. Oxygen—there had to be air.

He needed to add air. He had to fan on it, blow on it.

He made the nest ready again, held the hatchet backward, tensed, and struck four quick blows. Sparks came down and he leaned forward as fast as he could and blew.

Too hard. There was a bright, almost intense glow, then it was gone. He had blown it out.

Another set of strikes, more sparks. He leaned and blew, but gently this time, holding back and aiming the stream of air from his mouth to hit the brightest spot. Five or six sparks had fallen in a tight mass of bark hair and Brian centered his efforts there.

The sparks grew with his gentle breath. The red glow moved from the sparks themselves into the bark, moved and grew and became worms, glowing red worms that crawled up the bark hairs and caught other threads of bark and grew until there was a pocket of red as big as a quarter, a glowing red coal of heat.

And when he ran out of breath and paused to inhale, the red ball suddenly burst into flame.

"Fire!" He yelled. "I've got fire! I've got it, I've got it, I've got it . . ."

But the flames were thick and oily and burning fast, consuming the ball of bark as fast as if it were gasoline. He had to feed the flames, keep them going. Working as fast as he could he carefully placed the dried grass and wood pieces he had tried at first on top of the bark and was gratified to see them take.

But they would go fast. He needed more, and more. He could not let the flames go out.

He ran from the shelter to the pines and started breaking off the low, dead small limbs. These he threw in the shelter, went back for more, threw those in, and squatted to break and feed the hungry flames. When the small wood was going well he went out and found larger wood and did not relax until that was going.

Then he leaned back against the wood brace of his door opening and smiled.

I have a friend, he thought—I have a friend now. A hungry friend, but a good one. I have a friend named fire.

"Hello, fire . . ."

The curve of the rock back made an almost perfect drawing flue that carried the smoke up through the cracks of the roof but held the heat If he kept the fire small it would be perfect and would keep anything like the porcupine from coming through the door again.

A friend and a guard, he thought.

So much from a little spark. A friend and a guard from a tiny spark.

Gary Paulsen

The Joy of Fire

by Gary Paulsen

During the 1983 Iditarod, the annual sled dog race from Anchorage to Nome, Alaska, there came a time when a fire was very important to me. It was twenty degrees below zero, and I went through the ice on a river. I was tied to the sled with a short rope, and the dogs dragged me out, but I was soaked and the freezing process began immediately. Within twenty or thirty seconds, I couldn't work my fingers. In moments, I could barely move, could not even crawl to the dogs to huddle with them for warmth.

I had dry matches in the sled, so I opened the packet and jammed two matches between the fingers on my right hand. I scratched them to get them going. Near me was a dead, dry willow brush with fluffs of bark hanging down. When I put the match under the fluffs, they lit. I found small dead wood nearby and fed the flames—I was nearly screaming with joy by this time. Soon I had a fire to thaw my clothes enough to get them off (they had frozen to me) and then to stay warm enough to get into fresh clothing. There was tremendous luck involved. Had the matches not been handy in the sled, had I not been able to jam some in between my fingers and get them to light, or had there not been the dead willow with bark in hanging strips close by, I would have gone into hypothermia, or critically low body temperature. I would have died, I think, within minutes.

I thought about my experience during the Iditarod when I was writing about building a fire in *Hatchet.* I remembered how wonderful that was, the fire, how incredible it was to discover, to *know* fire. It is a strange feeling: to know that you will die if you do not get this fire, to absolutely know that, and then have the fire come for you, save you. I can still feel it, sitting now writing this—the joy of that heat, that friend, those flames. Brian would have felt the same joy, which I hope comes through in the book.

Pulling It All Together

1

As you read this story, what did you remember? What one event stands out in your memory? Why this particular event?

2

Here's a panel: Lemon Brown, Anne Frank, and Sweetgrass. Have them talk about what they had to face, how they faced their difficulties, and what advice they would have for you!

3

Everyone needs heroes, and heroes are often those who face danger with courage. Everyone needs his or her own personal Hall of Fame. What three heroes will you start with—your first three stops in your own personal Hall of Fame? And why do you choose those three?

Books to Enjoy

The Upstairs Room
by Johanna Reiss
Harper, 1972
Annie and her older sister Sini have to leave their mother, father, and older sister to hide from the Nazis in the upstairs room of the Oostervelds' farmhouse. People say that World War II can't last for long, but for two long years in the cramped little room, the war seems to go on and on. Will Annie, Sini, and the Oostervelds be found and sent to concentration camps?

No Way Out
by Ivy Ruckman
Harper, 1988
Amy thinks her ideal weekend will be spent hiking the Zion Narrows with her boyfriend Rick and her little brother Ben. When Amy decides to spend the night camping with some other hikers, Rick and Ben go off to rough it on their own. Then a flash flood upstream turns their outing into a nightmare of survival! Will they find each other in this rushing wall of water? Can they find a way out of the canyon?

Jackie Robinson
by John Grabowski
Chelsea House, 1991
Jackie Robinson was Branch Rickey's "great experiment." The owner of the Brooklyn Dodgers decided in 1947 that African Americans could and should play baseball in the major leagues. Many records later, Jackie Robinson was inducted into the Hall of Fame in 1962.

Would You Settle for Improbable?
by P. J. Petersen
Delacorte, 1981
Student teacher, "King Kong" Karnisian, has an unusual request for her class: Would her students befriend newcomer Arnold, recently released from Juvenile Hall? Will the class survive?

A Solitary Blue
by Cynthia Voigt
Atheneum, 1983
His mother leaves him when he's seven. His father is too self-absorbed to meet his needs. Then, when he's almost twelve, his activist-mother spends a summer with Jeff that changes his whole life. But is it for the better?

Children of the River
by Linda Crew
Delacorte, 1989
Uprooted by a bloody civil war, Sundara flees Cambodia with members of her family and tries to settle down in America. It isn't always easy balancing Cambodian ways and the new American ways, but Jonathan is there to help her.

Literary Terms

Biography A **biography** is the nonfiction story of a person's life written by someone else. A **biography** may cover part or all of the life of that person. "Happy Birthday, Anne" is a **biography** of Anne Frank's life during part of 1942.

Dialogue **Dialogue** is the conversation between characters in a story or a play. In drama, the story is told entirely through the **dialogue** (words) and actions of the actors, as it is in *The Diary of Anne Frank.* In fiction, stories use the comments of a narrator as well. In both plays and stories, the **dialogue** between characters reveals their feelings toward people and events in the story.

Diary A **diary** is a personal, day-to-day record of someone's thoughts about the events of his or her life. **Diaries** are most often not intended for publication, although some of them do get published. **Diary** entries show the dates they were recorded. "Good at Heart" is a section of Anne Frank's **diary.** After Anne died, her **diary** was found and published.

Drama A **drama,** or play, is a story written to be acted out. The story is told through the characters' words and actions. Stage directions, written in parentheses, tell the actors how to deliver their lines and how to move around on the stage. *The Diary of Anne Frank* is a **drama.** The stage directions tell the actress playing Anne to scream and moan as she wakes up from her nightmare. They also tell how the other characters should respond.

Idiom An **idiom** is a phrase or expression whose meaning cannot be understood from the ordinary meanings of the words that form it. For example in the theater if you say "break a leg" to an actor, you are telling him to do well in his performance. In "Eddie," Lonnie calls Eddie "dude" and "turkey." Those expressions are **idioms** because they have meanings that are different from the usual meanings of the words. **Idioms** are very difficult for people who are learning English as a new language because the word meanings in an **idiom** are different from the dictionary meanings.

Mood The atmosphere or feeling of a written work is its **mood.** The **mood** may reflect any emotion and may change during the story. Authors create **mood** by their choice of setting, objects, details, images, and words. The **mood** of "The Treasure of Lemon Brown" is frightening. When Greg pushes open the door to the old, empty building, there is a feeling of danger and fear. As Greg realizes that there is someone in the room with him, and when the thugs break into the building, the **mood** of fear increases.

Glossary

Vocabulary from your selections

ab surd (ab sėrd′, ab zėrd′), *adj.* plainly not true, logical, or sensible; ridiculous. **—ab surd′ly,** *adv.* **—ab surd′ness,** *n.*

au tism (ô′tiz′əm), *n.* (in psychology) condition in which a person is withdrawn and unresponsive and appears to be almost completely absorbed with the self. [< Greek *autos* self]

au tis tic (ô tis′tik), *adj.* **1** of or having to do with autism. **2** suffering from, or exhibiting symptoms of, autism. The **autistic child** may also be mute and be disturbed by changes in the physical environment.

beck on (bek′ən), *v.i., v.t.* to signal by a motion of the head or hand: *He beckoned me to follow him. The tall man beckoned to her.* [Old English *bēcnan* < *bēacen* sign, beacon]

bliss ful (blis′fəl), *adj.* supremely happy; joyful. **—bliss′ful ly,** *adv.* **—bliss′ful ness,** *n.*

bo de ga (bō dā′gə), *n.* a grocery store in a Spanish-speaking neighborhood.

cin e ma (sin′ə mə), *n.* **1** a motion picture. **2** a motion-picture theater. **3 the cinema,** motion pictures.

com mence (kə mens′), *v.,* **-menced, -menc ing.** *—v.i.* make a start; begin. *—v.t.* begin (an action); enter upon: *commence legal action.* **—com menc′er,** *n.*

crouch (krouch), *v.i.* **1** stoop low with bent legs like an animal ready to spring. **2** shrink down in fear. **3** bow down in a timid or slavish manner; cower. *—v.t.* bend low. *—n.* **1** act or state of crouching. **2** a crouching position.

de liv er ance (di liv′ər əns), *n.* **1** a setting free or a being set free; rescue; release. **2** a formal opinion or judgment.

de test (di test′), *v.t.* dislike intensely; hate. [< Latin *detestari* curse while calling the gods to witness < *de-* + *testis* witness] **—de test′er,** *n.*

endanger The bull **endangered** the bullfighter's life.

en dan ger (en dān′jər), *v.t.* cause danger to; expose to loss or injury; imperil: *Fire endangered the hotel's guests.*

ex as pe ra tion (eg zas′pə rā′shən), *n.* extreme annoyance; irritation; anger.

fa tal ism (fā′tl iz′əm), *n.* **1** belief that fate controls everything that happens. **2** acceptance of everything that happens because of this belief.

fa tal ist (fā′tl ist), *n.* believer in fatalism.

glow er (glou′ər), *v.i.* stare angrily; scowl fiercely: *The rivals glowered at each other.* —*n.* an angry stare; fierce scowl. **—glow′er ing ly,** *adv.*

hob ble (hob′əl), *v.,* **-bled, -bling,** *n.* —*v.i.* **1** walk awkwardly or lamely; limp. **2** move unsteadily. —*v.t.* **1** cause to walk awkwardly or limp. **2** tie the legs of (a horse, etc.) together in order to prevent free motion. **3** hinder. —*n.* **1** an awkward walk; limp. **2** rope or strap used to hobble a horse, etc. **—hob′bler,** *n.*

ig nite (ig nīt′), *v.,* **-nit ed, -nit ing.** —*v.t.* **1** set on fire: *She ignited the heap of rubbish.* **2** make intensely hot; cause to glow with heat. —*v.i.* take fire; begin to burn: *Gasoline ignites easily.* **—ig nit′a ble, ig nit′i ble,** *adj.* **—ig nit′er,** *n.*

im plore (im plôr′, im plōr′), *v.t.,* **-plored, -plor ing.** **1** beg or pray earnestly for. **2** beg (a person) to do something. **—im plor′er,** *n.* **—im plor′ing ly,** *adv.*

im promp tu (im promp′tü, im promp′tyü), *adv.* without previous thought or preparation; offhand: *a speech made impromptu.* —*adj.* made or done without previous thought or preparation: *an impromptu speech, an impromptu party.* —*n.* something made or done without previous thought or preparation; improvisation.

im pro vise (im′prə vīz), *v.,* **-vised, -vis ing.** —*v.t.* **1** make up (music, poetry, etc.) on the spur of the moment; sing, recite, speak, etc., without preparation. **2** provide offhand; make for the occasion: *The stranded motorists improvised a tent out of two blankets and some long poles.* —*v.i.* compose, utter, or do anything without preparation or on the spur of the moment. **—im′pro vis′er,** *n.*

im pu dent (im′pyə dənt), *adj.* shamelessly bold; very rude and insolent. [< Latin *impudentem* < *in-* not + *pudere* be modest] **—im′pu dent ly,** *adv.*

in tim i date (in tim′ə dāt), *v.t.,* **-dat ed, -dat ing.** **1** make afraid; frighten: *intimidate one's opponents with threats.* **2** influence or force by fear: *intimidate a witness.* **—in tim′i da′tion,** *n.* **—in tim′i da′tor,** *n.*

ju bi la tion (jü′bə lā′shən), *n.* **1** a rejoicing. **2** a joyful celebration.

a	hat	**oi**	oil
ā	age	**ou**	out
ä	far	**u**	cup
e	let	**ů**	put
ē	equal	**ü**	rule
ėr	term		
i	it	**ch**	child
ī	ice	**ng**	long
o	hot	**sh**	she
ō	open	**th**	thin
ô	order	**ᴛʜ**	then
		zh	measure

ə = a in about, e in taken, i in pencil, o in lemon, u in circus

< = derived from

glower He **glowered** at me as I passed.

jubilation The new toy filled the child with **jubilation.**

kin dling (kind′ling), *n.* small pieces of wood, etc., that ignite easily for setting fire to larger pieces and other fuel.

mount (mount), *v.t.* **1** go up on or climb up; ascend: *mount a hill, mount a ladder, mount stairs.* **2** get up on: *mount a horse, mount a platform.* **3** put on a horse, etc.; furnish with a horse or other animal for riding: *Some police in this city are mounted.* **4** put or fix in proper position or order for use: *mount specimens on a slide.* **5** fix in a setting, backing, support, etc.: *mount gems in gold, mount a picture on cardboard.* **6** carry or place (guns) in position for use, as a fortress or ship. **7** provide (a play) with scenery, costumes, properties, etc. **8** assign (a guard) as a sentry or watch. —*v.i.* **1** move or proceed upward. **2** rise in amount; increase; rise: *The cost of living mounts steadily.* **3** get on a horse, etc.; get up on something: *mount and ride away.* —*n.* **1** horse, bicycle, etc., provided for riding. **2** something in or on which anything is mounted; setting; backing; support: *a mount for microscopic examination.* —**mount′a ble,** *adj.*

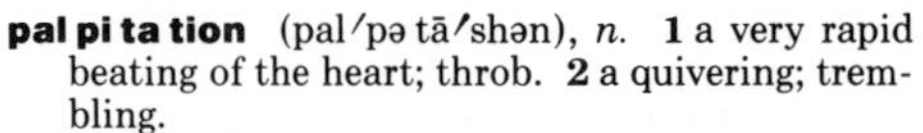

pal pi ta tion (pal′pə tā′shən), *n.* **1** a very rapid beating of the heart; throb. **2** a quivering; trembling.

physical therapy, treatment of diseases and defects by physical remedies, such as exercise and massage, rather than by drugs; physiotherapy.

recede The water **receded** at low tide.

re cede (ri sēd′), *v.i.,* **-ced ed, -ced ing. 1** go or move backward. **2** slope backward: *a chin that recedes.* **3** withdraw: *recede from an agreement.*

re strain (ri strān′), *v.t.* **1** hold back; keep in check or keep within limits; repress; curb: *I could not restrain my curiosity.* **2** keep in prison; confine. —**re strain′a ble,** *adj.* —**re strain′ed ly,** *adv.* —**re strain′er,** *n.*

self-pit y (self′pit′ē), *n.* pity for oneself.

short-hand ed (shôrt′han′did), *adj.* not having enough workers, helpers, etc.: *We were short-handed at the store today. Also* **shorthanded.**

skit ter (skit′ər), *v.i.* move lightly or quickly; skim or skip along a surface. —*v.t.* cause to skitter.

stark (stärk), *adj.* **1** downright; complete; sheer: *That fool is talking stark nonsense.* **2** stiff; rigid: *The dog lay stark in death.* **3** bare; barren; desolate: *a stark landscape.* **4** harsh; stern. **5** ARCHAIC. strong; sturdy. —*adv.* **1** entirely; completely: *stark, raving mad.* **2** in a stark manner. —**stark′ly,** *adv.* —**stark′ness,** *n.*

stoop (stüp), *n.* porch or platform at the entrance of a house.

ten dril (ten′drəl), *n.* **1** a thread-like part of a climbing plant that attaches itself to something and helps support the plant. **2** something similar: *curly tendrils of hair.*

tense (tens), *adj.,* **tens er, tens est,** *v.,* **tensed, tens ing.** —*adj.* **1** stretched tight; strained to stiffness: *a tense rope, a face tense with pain.* **2** keyed up; strained: *tense nerves, a tense moment.* **3** (in phonetics) pronounced with the muscles of the speech organs relatively tense. —*v.t., v.i.* stretch tight; tighten; stiffen: *I tensed my muscles for the leap.* **—tense′ly,** *adv.* **—tense′ness,** *n.*

ten ta tive (ten′tə tiv), *adj.* **1** done as a trial or experiment; experimental: *We made tentative plans to work together for six months.* **2** hesitating: *Her tentative laugh indicated that she hadn't understood the joke.* **—ten′ta tive-ly,** *adv.* **—ten′ta tive ness,** *n.*

thrive (thrīv), *v.i.,* **throve** or **thrived, thrived** or **thriv en** (thriv′ən), **thriv ing. 1** grow or develop well; grow vigorously: *Flowers will not thrive without sunshine.* **2** be successful; grow rich; prosper. **—thriv′er,** *n.* **—thriv′ing ly,** *adv.*

tin der (tin′dər), *n.* **1** anything that catches fire easily. **2** material used to catch fire from a spark.

tran quil (trang′kwəl), *adj.,* **-quil er, -quil est** or **-quil ler, -quil lest.** free from agitation or disturbance; calm; peaceful; quiet. **—tran′quil ly,** *adv.* **—tran′quil ness,** *n.*

tran quil li ty or **tran quil i ty** (trang kwil′ə tē), *n.* tranquil condition; calmness; peacefulness; quiet.

un daunt ed (un dôn′tid, un dän′tid), *adj.* not afraid; not dismayed or discouraged; fearless. **—un daunt′ed ly,** *adv.* **—un daunt′ed-ness,** *n.*

vast (vast), *adj.* very great; immense: *Texas and Alaska cover vast territories. A billion dollars is a vast amount.* —*n.* an immense space. **—vast′ly,** *adv.* **—vast′ness,** *n.*

what not (hwot′not′, hwut′not′), *n.* a stand with several shelves for books, ornaments, etc.

with drawn (wiᴛʜ drôn′, with drôn′), *v.* pp. of **withdraw.** —*adj.* **1** retiring; reserved; shy. **2** isolated; secluded.

wrought (rôt), *adj.* **1** made: *The gate was wrought with great skill.* **2** formed with care; not rough or crude. **3** manufactured or treated; not in a raw state. **4** (of metals or metalwork) formed by hammering.

a	hat	**oi**	oil
ā	age	**ou**	out
ä	far	**u**	cup
e	let	**u̇**	put
ē	equal	**ü**	rule
ėr	term		
i	it	**ch**	child
ī	ice	**ng**	long
o	hot	**sh**	she
ō	open	**th**	thin
ô	order	**ᴛʜ**	then
		zh	measure
		ə =	a in about
			e in taken
			i in pencil
			o in lemon
			u in circus
		< =	derived from

tranquillity The lake gave a feeling of **tranquillity.**

Acknowledgments

Text

Page 7: From *The Outside Shot* by Walter Dean Myers. Copyright © 1984 by John Ballard. Used by permission of Dell Books, a division of Bantam Doubleday Dell Publishing Group, Inc.
Page 23: "The Treasure of Lemon Brown" by Walter Dean Myers. Copyright © 1983 by Walter Dean Myers. Reprinted by permission of the author.
Page 39: "Writing and Revising 'The Treasure of Lemon Brown'" by Walter Dean Myers. Copyright © by Walter Dean Myers, 1991.
Page 44: "Wealth" by Tony Moreno from *Of Stone and Tears*, published by The Greenfield Review Press, Greenfield Center, New York. Reprinted by permission.
Page 45: "First Star" by Eve Merriam from *If Only I Could Tell You* by Eve Merriam. Copyright © 1983 by Eve Merriam. Reprinted by permission of Marian Reiner for the author.
Page 47: Excerpt from *Anne Frank: Life in Hiding* by Johanna Hurwitz. Text copyright © 1988 by Johanna Hurwitz. Reprinted by permission of The Jewish Publication Society.
Page 67: From *The Diary of Anne Frank* by Frances Goodrich and Albert Hackett. Copyright 1954, 1956 as an unpublished work. Copyright © 1956 by Albert Hackett, Frances Goodrich Hackett and Otto Frank. Reprinted by permission of Random House, Inc. *Caution: The Diary of Anne Frank* is the sole property of the dramatists and is fully protected by copyright. It may not be acted by professionals or amateurs without written permission and the payment of a royalty. All rights, including professional, amateur, stock, radio broadcasting, television, motion picture, recitation, lecturing, public reading, and the rights of translation into foreign languages, are reserved. All inquiries should be addressed to the dramatists' agent: Leah Salisbury, 234 West 44th Street, New York.
Page 85: Excerpts from *Anne Frank: The Diary of a Young Girl* by Anne Frank. Copyright 1952 by Otto H. Frank. Used by permission of Doubleday, a division of Bantam Doubleday Dell Publishing Group, Inc. and Valentine, Mitchell Co. Ltd.
Page 92: "Dream Variation" from *Selected Poems* by Langston Hughes. Copyright 1926 by Alfred A. Knopf, Inc. and renewed 1954 by Langston Hughes. Reprinted by permission of the publisher.
Pages 92–93: "Dreams" and "The Dream Keeper" from *The Dream Keeper and Other Poems* by Langston Hughes. Copyright 1932 by Alfred A. Knopf, Inc. and renewed 1960 by Langston Hughes. Reprinted by permission of the publisher.
Page 93: "Dream Deferred" from *The Panther and the Lash* by Langston Hughes. Copyright 1951 by Langston Hughes. Reprinted by permission of Alfred A. Knopf, Inc.
Page 95: "The River Demon" by Jan Hudson from *Sweetgrass*. Copyright © 1984 by Jan Hudson. Reprinted by permission of Philomel Books and Tree Frog Press, Canada.
Page 117: From *Hatchet* by Gary Paulsen. Text copyright © 1987 by Gary Paulsen. Reprinted with permission of Bradbury Press, an affiliate of Macmillan, Inc.
Page 133: "The Joy of Fire" by Gary Paulsen. Copyright by Gary Paulsen, 1991.

Artists

Illustrations owned and copyrighted by the illustrator.
David Diaz: Cover, 1, 3, 135, 136, 138
Norman Cousineau: 44, 45, 92, 93
Mary Flock: 46, 65, 66, 67, 83, 84, 91
Debbie Drechsler: 94, 95, 115, 116–117, 120, 121, 123, 125, 126, 129, 134
Corwin Pearson: 132

Photographs

Pages 6, 14, 22–37: Peter Rosenbaum
Page 38: Courtesy of Walter Dean Myers
Pages 47, 51, 57, 58, 60, 63: Anne Frank-Fonds/Cosmopress, Geneve
Page 54: Loomis Dean, Life Magazine Time Warner Inc., courtesy Otto Frank
Page 132: Art based on photo courtesy of Gary Paulsen

Glossary

The contents of the Glossary entries in this book have been adapted from Scott Foresman *Advanced Dictionary*, copyright © 1988 by Scott, Foresman and Company.
Page 140: Walter S. Clark, Jr.; Page 141 (top): E.M. Demjen/Stock Boston, Inc.; Page 141 (bottom): Gretchen Garner; Page 142: Nova Scotia Information Service; Page 143: Wayne Lankinen/Bruce Coleman, Inc.
Unless otherwise acknowledged, all photographs are the property of ScottForesman.